MAKING PICTURE FRAMES IN WOOD

MAKING PICTURE FRAMES IN WOOD

Manly Banister

 Sterling Publishing Co., Inc.   New York

Library of Congress Cataloging in Publication Data

Banister, Manly Miles, 1914–
  Making picture frames in wood.

  (Home craftsman series)
  Revision of: Making picture frames.   1973.
  Includes index.
  1. Picture frames and framing.   I. Title.
N8550.B35   1981   749'.7   81-50985
ISBN 0-8069-5450-7   AACR2
ISBN 0-8069-5451-5 (lib. bdg.)
ISBN 0-8069-7542-3 (pbk.)

      15   17   19   20   18   16

Copyright © 1982 by Sterling Publishing Co., Inc.
387 Park Avenue South, New York, N.Y. 10016
Distributed in Canada by Sterling Publishing
% Canadian Manda Group, P.O. Box 920, Station U
Toronto, Ontario, Canada M8Z 5P9
Distributed in Great Britain and Europe by Cassell PLC
Artillery House, Artillery Row, London SW1P 1RT, England
Distributed in Australia by Capricorn Ltd.
P.O. Box 665, Lane Cove, NSW 2066
Manufactured in the United States of America

Contents

Before

You

Begin

Cave painters, perhaps the first "artists" in history, did not put frames around their works. Today, however, frame-making is almost as highly developed an art as painting itself.

Why We Use Frames

Often, a frame serves as a line of separation between the activity of the painting and the wall upon which it is hung. By segregating the art from its surround, the frame focuses the viewer's attention directly upon the art and not its environment.

But not all modern frames are merely thin lines of demarcation. Frames can be—and often are—crafted with a character of their own, yet a character that is always secondary to the picture itself.

How To Choose a Frame

There are no rules for choosing a frame for a given picture. Your own personal preferences and good taste should be your guide in your selections. If you feel that a given frame and picture go together, you're probably right.

However, as a general rule, it is customary to use simple, narrow

Illus. 1. Two ancient rulers of Egypt grace a double window gilt mat. The frame is carved with a round file and textured with a comb drawn through thick gesso.

frames with matted prints, watercolors and reproductions. Large paintings can "carry" the bulk of wider, deeper frames that can even be carved and gilded to enhance their appearance.

Why Make Your Own Picture Frames?

First and foremost, frame-making is an esteemed craft that offers both the amateur and the highly skilled artisan a rewarding creative outlet. You can choose for yourself just how much effort—and money—you want to expend. You can start from "scratch," moulding and shaping ordinary flat lumber in almost any way you desire, producing a picture-frame moulding that is unlike any other—and in some cases, more artistic and creative than the picture itself!

If you yourself are a professional or amateur artist, you may want the entire project to be your own creation, in which case you'll want to make your own frames, as well. Here, you'll find ideas for matting and framing prints, watercolors, oil and acrylic paintings, ceramics, you name it!

Starting with prefinished frames which require only preparing the art for the beginner, you can move on to ready-made but unfinished frames from your local variety store that you can carve, shape and finish yourself. Or, you can create and assemble the frame with the simple power tools common to every home workshop: a radial-arm or bench saw, a router, a few rasps and files, a miter box, hammers, pliers and so on. Then you can finish with paints and gilt.

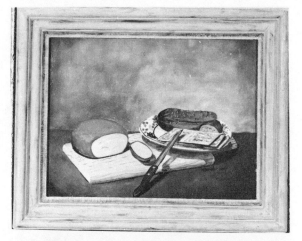

Illus. 2. This attractive frame is a lot simpler to make than it looks. Made from 1 × 2 moulded to the shape shown in profile 24 (page 76), it was daubed with acrylic modelling paste in the wide gully, painted red and gilded. Inner rim was textured with a comb.

Illus. 3. To make this frame, look at profile 47 (page 86) and paint with acrylics, gild, and texture.

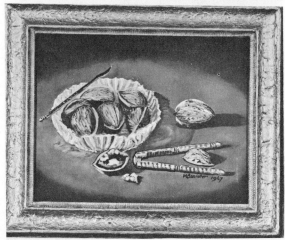

Illus. 4. This still life looks most appropriate in a textured and gilded frame made from profile 46 (page 87).

Mounting the Artwork

Mounting for Different Types of Art

Original Prints, Drawings and Watercolors

Original artwork executed on paper that possesses some value (whether monetary ánd/or sentimental) should be preserved. The first step in its care and preservation is mounting, that is, the attaching of the artwork to a backing or support.

Never stick fine art down with glue or dry-mounting tissue. The idea is to mount it securely enough so that it will not slip after it is framed, but so that it also can be demounted without difficulty (for changing the mount and/or frame).

Always handle original art carefully—by the edges only so as not to smudge it with fingerprints. Don't drop, wrinkle, bend, or fold a piece of art as all these may decrease or destroy its value.

Both the mat and the mounting board must be of 100-percent-rag constitution (museum board). Museum board is so called because it is used by art museums for mounting art. If the artwork were mounted on standard matboard, its acids might diffuse out from the edges of the window and stain the paper support of the art, spoiling its appearance, and, consequently its value. So, never use a paper or board that you do not *know* is 100-percent-rag and acid-free.

Mounting Photographs and Reproductions

For ordinary work such as photographs and reproductions, you can use standard matboard with only a few reservations. The paper adhered to the board is reasonably acid-free, so you will gain a measure of protection by painting all cut edges with acrylic matte medium—window edges can be painted with acrylic colors if desired. The acrylics seal the edges and add to the life of the art.

Museum board is, of course, more expensive than standard matboard and usually is available only in white and cream color, with a choice of possibly only a few other colors. To have a colored mat, you can either paint the museum board mat, or double-mat the art with a top mat of standard matboard of whatever color you desire.

Mounting Techniques

Wet Mounting

Pasting or gluing the art to the mounting board is called "wet mounting." Small reproductions, magazine cutouts and photos of little value are usually wet-mounted.

A non-warping glue, available at art supply stores and used for mounting, may be thinned with water for easier brushing. It is called Yes Glue. Brush a thin coat on the back of the art (spreading newspapers on the table). Also, keep a damp towel and a dry towel handy; you will get glue on your hands and will want to wipe it off quickly to keep from soiling the art with it. Only a thin coat is needed; if it is too thick, scrape off the excess with a narrow spatula or a piece of lattice moulding.

First, assemble the mat to the mounting board (Illus. 5). Hinge the mat and the board together at the top with a strip of linen tape. With the mat closed, mark the location of the two upper corners of the window on the mounting board. From there, measure out the exact location of the art and mark the upper corners with intersecting lines. Lay the glued artwork in place and press it down, then roll it with a soft rubber roller (Illus. 6) to ensure adhesion.

If you use a spray adhesive, follow the directions on the can. If you must use ordinary paste, get some wallpaper paste powder from a hardware dealer. Mix a small amount with water. Be aware, however, that this

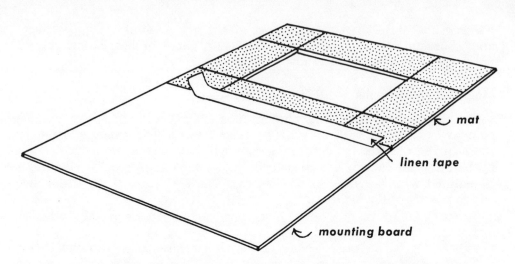

Illus. 5. To assemble the mat, lay top edges of mat and mounting board together and join them with linen tape.

Illus. 6. When mounting a photo with spray adhesive, roll over the print with a soft rubber roller (inking roller) to avoid damage to the emulsion.

will undoubtedly warp the mounting board, a condition that is cured by "countermounting." Paste a backing of Kraft wrapping paper with the same paste on the other side of the board to pull it straight again. Place between waxed paper and under a piece of plywood weighted down until the paste dries; overnight is best.

Dry Mounting

Dry mounting is so called because there is no moisture involved. It is done with "dry-mounting tissue," available at photo supply or art supply shops. Whether mounted with a mat or not, photographs and trimmed art of little value are often dry-mounted. A trimmed photo or picture can be mounted and the mat window cut large to allow ¼ in (6.4 mm) or so of the mounting board to show all around as an element of separation. However, do not dry-mount any photo or work of art of monetary value. Sticking art all over to the mounting board destroys its value. Such work should be mounted as described in Chapter 2 for fine art.

Dry-mounting tissue is made with a thermosetting adhesive on both sides. When heated, the tissue bonds to the back of the art and to the mounting board. The heat can be applied either by a dry-mounting press or by a household electric iron. With practice, you can successfully dry-mount double-weight prints up to 16 × 20 in (40.6 × 50.8 cm) in size, using only an electric iron.

Standard dry-mounting tissue melts and bonds at 225°F (107°C) and is used for bonding reproductions, magazine cutouts, construction or fancily patterned paper, photos on standard photographic paper, or anything else that is not resin-coated photographic paper. Such coated paper requires use of a special tissue that bonds at a lower temperature, as too much heat will damage a picture on resin-coated paper. Ask your dealer specifically for it. This tissue also will bond all other materials, so you can use it for everything. (Be sure to drain the water out of your steam iron, as steam is neither needed nor desirable.)

First, make a pad of newspaper about ½ in (12.7 mm) thick and cover it with a piece of Kraft wrapping paper. Lay the mounting board on the pile and iron it on both sides with a medium heat to drive out any moisture that may be present.

Do it this way: Cut a piece of tissue the size of the art. Lay the art face-down and the tissue on top. With a dry-mount tacking iron set at slightly more than medium heat, or the tip of an electric iron set at the heat for nylon or silk, tack the tissue along one edge of the art in a continuous line about 3 in (7.6 cm) long, at the middle of the edge (Illus. 7). Any adhesive that sticks to your iron can be removed with a cloth dampened with lacquer thinner. You can also buy release paper to which the tissue will not stick, and insert it between the tacking iron and the tissue.

Having prepared the mat for mounting the art, position it and cover with Kraft paper to protect it from direct contact with the iron. With the heat set at "wool" or "low" (you now have to heat through the art paper to melt the adhesive on the tissue), tack the *opposite side* of the art to the mounting board (Illus. 8).

Lay on a sheet of Kraft paper over the whole mount and proceed to iron the entire area (Illus. 9). *Keep the iron moving.* Iron fanwise from the mount tack outward. Turn the mount over and iron it all over from the back. Then turn back to the front and iron some more. Continue, alternating a few times, until mount and art are hot and adhere. Then, before it has a chance to cool, lay the mat on a cool, flat surface, cover it with a piece of hardboard and weight it down. Leave it there until it thoroughly cools. Special twin weights from a photo supply house are ideal for weighting; they are steel plates weighing 10 lbs (4.5 kg) apiece and fit together so one can be used on top of the other. You can also use yellow fire bricks. These weigh 7½ lbs (3.4 kg) apiece and can be purchased at a building supply firm. They are inexpensive and can be lacquered to keep them from giving off a fine dust. Glue cork or felt to the bottom to prevent scratching and you can epoxy a handle on top if desired. A half-dozen of these will come in handy.

Mounting with Linen Hinges

Fine art is invariably attached to the mounting board with a hinge at each top corner (Illus. 10). Usually, this is Holland cloth linen tape. The same tape is used in fastening mat and mounting board together. These are laid out top to top and the tape is moistened, then rubbed down over the joint. If a double mat is being assembled, attach the bottom mat to the mounting board in this manner, then attach the top mat to the bottom mat (Illus. 11).

Watercolors, etchings and lithographs executed on heavy paper are usually mounted as in Illus. 10. First, locate the corners of the paper support and mark them on the mounting board as follows: Place the art on the mounting board and close the mat on it. Adjust the art to the opening and weight it down so it will stay put. Carefully open the mat and mark the two upper corners of the support on the mounting board with intersecting pencil lines. Remove the art and cut two 1-in (2.5-cm) lengths of adhesive-backed Holland cloth linen tape. Fold back a tab ⅛ in (3.2 cm) wide on each, moisten the gum on the remainder and stick the

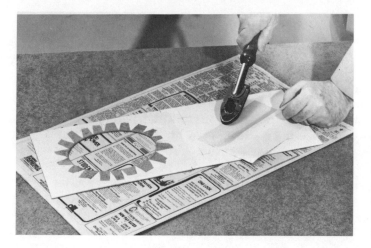

Illus. 7. Tack dry-mounting tissue to back of art along middle of one edge. Dry-mount tacking iron is in use here.

hinge down in the corner you have marked. Rub down the fold-over so that it lies flat. Moisten the fold-over on each hinge and carefully lay the art in place and rub it down on the hinges. Let set a short time for the gum to grab hold. You can now lift the art by its bottom edge and it should remain attached at the top to the mount.

If the time comes that the art is to be removed from the mount, simply moisten the joint between the hinge tab and the back of the art paper with a damp wad of cotton and the adhesive will let go.

The mat is now fixed to the mount to avoid any shifting of alignment while fitting (assembling the contents of the frame). You can space short pieces of double-stick tape around the mounting board and press the mat down against them for temporary holding. If you plan something more permanent, place a drop of Elmer's Glue-All, or a similar glue, every 2 in (5.1 cm) around the mount and close the mat. Place under a piece of plywood and plenty of weight and leave until the glue dries.

Determine beforehand, though, if the artwork causes the mat window to bulge outward, as may sometimes happen with a watercolor. If so, drop a little glue around the opening, but not touching the art, to keep the mat flat.

Mounting Artwork with Rice-Paper Support

A drawback of the method of hinging described above is that it may cause the paper to bulge if it is not heavy enough to maintain its shape. In such an event, an effective alternative is to use rice-paper hinges, or a special treatment with linen hinges.

15

After the mat has been assembled and the upper corners of the art located and marked on the mounting board, tear short lengths of rice paper about 1 in (2.5 cm) wide from a sheet. The torn edges will show less through the support. Lay the art face-down and stick the hinges to each corner with rice-flour paste, overlapping the art by no more than ⅛ in (3.2 mm). Give the hinges a chance to dry and stick, then position the art on the mounting board and stick down ⅛ in (3.2 mm) of the rice-paper hinges to the mount with rice-flour paste. Two hinges are enough, except in the case where it is large enough for the center to sag; in that case, apply a third hinge in the middle.

For a heavier paper, you can use linen tape in the same way. After ⅛ in (3.2 mm) of the end of the linen hinge is stuck to the back of the art and the art laid in place, you will see that the gummed side of the tape is upward. Cut this off ⅝ in (16 mm) long. Weight the art in place and cut a length of linen tape into ½-in (12.7-mm) widths and tape down the hinges ⅛ in (3.2 mm) from the art (Illus. 11A). If the space between the retaining tape and the art is more than this, it might stick to the back of the mat and some day cause embarrassment when you try to open it.

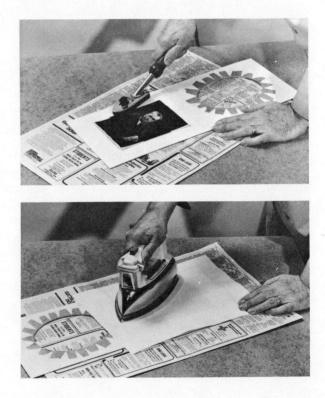

Illus. 8. Turn art over and tack opposite edge to the mounting board.

Illus. 9. For dry mounting, iron the mount on both sides with iron set at "wool." Heat adheres dry mounting tissue to the art and the mounting board.

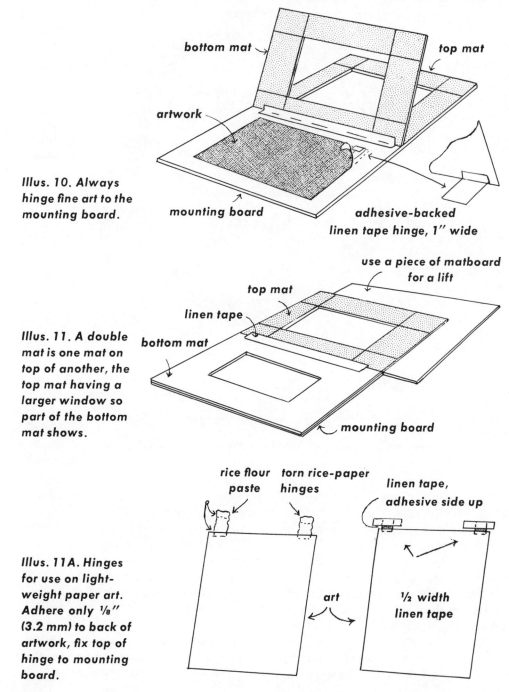

bottom mat

top mat

artwork

mounting board

**adhesive-backed
linen tape hinge, 1″ wide**

Illus. 10. Always hinge fine art to the mounting board.

**use a piece of matboard
for a lift**

top mat

linen tape

bottom mat

mounting board

Illus. 11. A double mat is one mat on top of another, the top mat having a larger window so part of the bottom mat shows.

**rice flour
paste**

**torn rice-paper
hinges**

**linen tape,
adhesive side up**

art

**½ width
linen tape**

Illus. 11A. Hinges for use on light-weight paper art. Adhere only ⅛″ (3.2 mm) to back of artwork, fix top of hinge to mounting board.

17

Cutting

and Covering

Mats

Mats: Preliminaries

A print may be temporarily matted and hung without benefit of frame, or it may be framed behind glass. Where it is intended to be up on a wall for a considerable length of time, or in a home where the air is full of cooking grease and household dust, the glassed frame is by all means the best way of preserving the print while it is displayed.

The place where the print is to be displayed is an important consideration in the case of a professional exhibit. Museums, galleries and art organizations have their own rules about the size and color of the mount and how it is to be hung. Therefore, you should approach the individual in charge of the exhibit in regard to these matters and never risk having your print rejected simply because it does not meet a few technical requirements in mounting.

For less formal exhibits, where no particular regulations are stipulated, the artist or frame-maker has considerable freedom in choosing the size and color of the mat. Only the canons of good taste impose limitations.

Temporary Mounting

In order to mat a print, you must secure a cardboard called matboard. It is made expressly for this purpose.

The entire mount consists of the matboard and a backing board to which the print is attached. Use illustration board for the latter, as its white surface reflects the light passing through the print and reinforces its contrasts. Under no circumstances use a dark-toned strawboard for a backing as it will make the print look dull.

Ordinary, inexpensive matboard and illustration board are satisfactory for temporary mounting. If the mounting is to be permanent, 100-percent-rag board should be used, both in the mat and in the backing. Museum board, available at art supply stores, is recommended. Whereas museum board is more expensive than ordinary matboard, it is your assurance that the mat will not decrease in attractiveness with time nor cause stains to appear on the margins of the print from chemicals and impurities, as may happen when a print is left in a mount of the cheaper board for an extended period of time. See Chapter 1.

The mat and the backing board are cut to size. The size, unless specified by a committee in charge of an exhibit, depends on your own taste and feelings, or upon the frame into which it must fit. No print should be jammed into a mount so that it has a crowded look, a result of skimpy margins on the mat. Even a small print should not have any margin less than an inch wide, nor should the largest print have a margin more than 5 or 6 inches (12.5 or 15 cm) in width.

Photography has made certain dimensions popular in this century, and we think of prints in sizes of 6 × 8, 8 × 10, 11 × 14, 14 × 17 and so on. The stock frames carried by art and variety stores are generally obtainable in these sizes. However, a print that is tall and thin, or one that is perfectly square, certainly presents mounting problems not encountered in the standard size. A narrow print naturally calls for narrower margins on the mat than one of wider dimensions. Therefore, it is important not to feel too restrained by the obligations of standard frame sizes.

If you intend to hang a matted print without a frame, you can secure it to the wall with a stick-on mat hanger, available at your art supply store. Stick the hanger to the back of the mat, positioned in the middle laterally and about 3 inches (7.5 cm) below the top edge. As soon as the glue on it has set, the print is ready to hang on the wall.

An unframed mat should not be allowed to hang for too long a time, however. Without a frame and glass to hold it flat, the mat will warp, particularly if it is hung near a heater.

Now to the specific tools you will need and the steps to follow.

Tools and Materials

◆ *Rules.* Illus. 6 and 7. Yardstick or metre stick, a 3 ft (.9-m) or 4 ft (1.2-m) aluminum rule, or 6 ft (1.8 m) folding wood rule. A steel tape should lock and be at least ¾ in (19 mm) wide for rigidity.

◆ *Square.* A carpenter's framing square for laying out mat openings; a 12-in (30-cm) square for checking rectangles. A 12-in (30-cm) combination square is handy for making measurements from the edge of the mat.

◆ *Straightedge.* Preferably of steel, ⅜ in (9.5 mm) thick, one edge beveled, one straight. A stainless-steel straightedge can be used.

◆ *Home-Built Mat-Cutting Jig.* (Illus. 15 and 16.) A long one for cutting across the width of a full sheet of matboard. A shorter one with easier handling for the cutting of smaller mats, especially when the straightedge needs to be clamped over the mat to hold it for two-handed bevel cutting. It has dowel-stops to keep the straightedge from slipping.

◆ *Mat Knives.* A number of different makes and designs of utility knives are on the market. You will find one or more at your hardware or art supply store. The Dexter multipurpose knife has a bent handle. All have replaceable blades and some have retractable blades. Keep blades razor-sharp by whetting on a Carborundum 102 razor hone or other fine stone (see below). Replace when point wears down.

◆ *X-Acto Knives or Single-Edge Razor Blades.* For fine trimming and making mat-window cuts into the corners.

◆ *Sharpening Stone.* Use a fine-textured stone. Most expensive is hard, white Arkansas stone. Use with oil or honing fluid, so make sure you clean it all off before cutting a mat. The Carborundum razor hone works well with water. A fine-grained India stone is also excellent.

◆ *Compass.* One that holds a pencil is fine, or use a regular drawing compass. For drawing guide circles for the cutting of circular mats.

◆ *Rubber Rollers.* A hard rubber print roller from an art or photo supply store and a soft rubber roller, such as is used for inking wood or linoleum blocks in printing. The latter won't mar photos.

◆ *Woodworker's Marking Gauge.* Replace the scratch-point with pencil lead and use it for marking out mat openings.

◆ *Scissors.* For cutting paper, cloth, trimming, and so on.

◆ *Circle Cutter.* A small one cuts circles to about an 8-in (20.3-cm)

Illus. 12. Some matting tools and materials. 1) Fire brick weight. 2) Adhesives. 3) Holland cloth linen tape. 4) Marking gauge. 5) Hard-and soft-rubber rollers. 6) Bone folder (on double roller). 7) Dexter mat cutter. 8) Carborundum Razor Hone #102. 9) Mat knives. 10) Locking steel tape. 11) 6' folding wood rule. 12) 12" steel square. 13) 12" stainless steel rule. 14) Carpenter's framing square. 15) Metre stick. 16) 48" aluminum rule.

diameter, but makes only a vertical cut. Bevel-cutting circle cutters can be purchased in sizes up to 40 in (1 m) diameter.

♦ *Watercolor Soft-Tip Pens.* A set provides a choice of colors for painting the bevelled edges of mat windows.

♦ *Jeweler's Metal-Cutting Snips.* One pair with straight blades and another with curved blades. For cutting out circles and ovals.

♦ *Weights.* When you have to weight something down, yellow fire bricks serve the purpose. Keep a half-dozen around. Paint them with Deft (a lacquer-type finish) to keep them from dusting, and glue cork or felt on the bottom so they won't scratch. You can also epoxy a handle on (Illus. 12).

♦ *Holland Cloth Tape.* An acid-free, adhesive-backed linen tape, 1 in (2.5 cm) wide, also 2 in (5.1 cm). For hinging artwork to the mounting board.

21

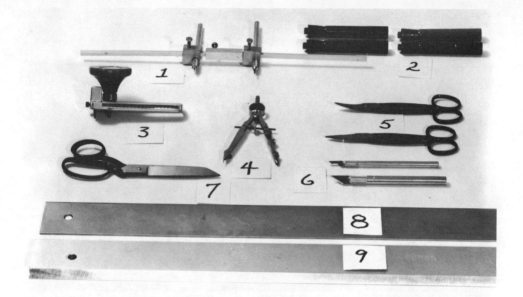

Illus. 13. More matting tools. 1) X-Acto beam circle cutter. 2) Soft-tip watercolor pens for cloring bevel edges of windows. 3) Circle cutter. 4) Compass. 5) Jeweler's metal snips. 6) X-Acto knives. 7) Scissors. 8) Stainless steel straightedge. 9) ⅜-" (9.5-mm)-thick steel straightedge.

♦ *Rice Paper*. Japanese paper, not made from rice but from wood of the mulberry tree. Tear, do not cut, into hinges for attaching flimsy or lightweight fine art to 100 percent-rag mounting board.

♦ *Glue, Spray Adhesive, Paste*. Yes Glue or Spray Adhesive from an art supply store, Elmer's Glue-All, and so on. Wallpaper paste is available in powdered form at hardware dealers.

♦ *Work Table*. You need one large enough—32 × 60 in (81.3 × 152 cm), if you have room for it. If your table proves to be too small, enlarge it by laying on a sheet of plywood cut to larger dimensions. Cover with ⅛ in (3.2 mm) hardboard for a smooth working surface.

Mat Styles and Matboards

Illus. 14 shows a few of the many possible ways to cut a mat. The openings can be used for photographs as well as for all kinds of artwork. Often the effect of the mat is enhanced if one or two lines are drawn around the window with a ruling pen, using black or colored India ink.

You can buy matboard in a wide range of colors at an art supply store.

Illus. 14. A few of the infinite number of mat styles you can create.

It comes $\frac{1}{16}$ in (1.5 mm) thick, 32 × 40 in (81.3 × 101.6 cm) in size. Larger sizes are available, but might require special order.

Original artwork on 100 percent-rag paper should be protected from acidic materials by mounting it on museum board and covering with a mat of museum board. Two coats of acrylic mat medium in the rabbet of the frame will help protect against the acid occurring naturally in wood. Museum board is available in white and cream colors (and possibly a few others) in 2-ply ($\frac{1}{32}$ in [1 mm]), 4-ply ($\frac{1}{16}$ in [1.5 mm], and up to 8-ply ($\frac{1}{8}$ in [3.2 mm]) board. The last named can be quite effective when bevel-cut. When no ply is specified in the text, 4-ply is to be understood. Museum board, to be so titled, must be of 100 percent-rag content and manufactured to certain government specifications for an acid-free board.

◆ *Mat Knives and the Mat-Cutting Jig.* Cutting a mat requires not only skill developed by practice, but also a razor-sharp mat knife and a heavy, wide straightedge, preferably $\frac{3}{8}$ in (10 mm) thick. Use of the jig (shown in Illus. 15–16) is recommended to ensure that the straightedge does not slip and spoil the cut.

Several styles of mat knives are available, all amounting to the same thing, for all are suitable. Take your choice. The Dexter Mat Cutter (Illus. 17) is one of several mat cutters of similar design. It is used with a straightedge for vertical and bevel cuts, but must be used freehand when cutting along a curved line. The knife is set back from the guiding edge, so allow space between the straightedge and the cutting line marked on the mat.

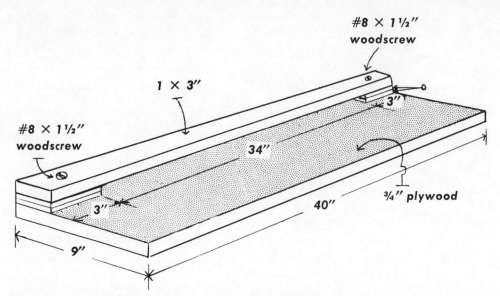

Illus. 15. Clamped to the work table with a C-clamp, this homemade jig keeps the straightedge from slipping, and is particularly useful for making bevel cuts.

Illus. 15 and 16 show two designs for an easy-to-build mat cutting jig. When clamped to the work table with a C-clamp, the jig keeps the straight-edge from being pushed aside by the knife. Use of the jig is essential in cutting a bevel.

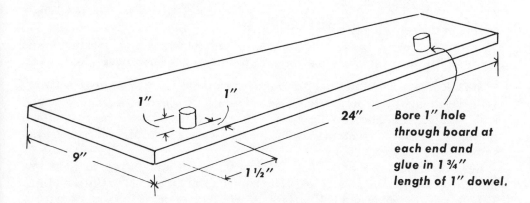

Illus. 16. Another design for a mat-cutting jig. Most useful where a thin straight-edge is clamped to the mat so that both hands can be used in making a bevel cut for greater accuracy.

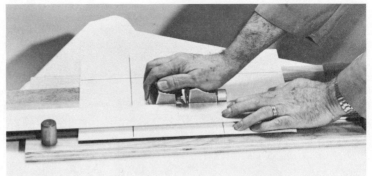

Illus. 17. Cutting a bevel with the Dexter Mat Cutter. Note that the straightedge lies across the mat margin. This photo also shows the dowel-stop mat-cutting jig in use.

What Color Mat?

To choose the right color mat, consider the colors in the art and whether they will harmonize or conflict with the mat color. The mat should never be more noticeable than the art. It must complement the art—that is, it should *complete* the art and give it a finished look.

A general rule is that the mat color may be the same as the main color scheme of the artwork or complementary to it. The best way to choose a mat color is to hold the art against it and see at a glance whether the two harmonize or clash.

You do not, of course, have a choice of an infinite number of colors when buying matboard, though more than several dozen are available. If you want a color not to be had in matboard, use white museum board and paint it with acrylic colors thinned with water to the consistency of watercolor. Acrylic paint is waterproof when dry.

The "color wheel" (Illus. 18) shows colors in their proper relationship to each other. There are three kinds of colors: (1) primary colors, (2) secondary colors, and (3) intermediate colors.

The primaries are red, yellow and blue. Mix red light with yellow and blue light and the result is white. But don't expect to get white by mixing colored pigments! The result is mud.

There are three secondary colors, made by mixing equal quantities of two adjacent primaries:

Yellow + blue = green.

Blue + red = violet or purple.

Red + yellow = orange.

There are six intermediate colors, one between each pair of primary and secondary colors: red–orange, blue–green, red–violet or magenta.

Colors directly opposite each other on the wheel are called "comple-

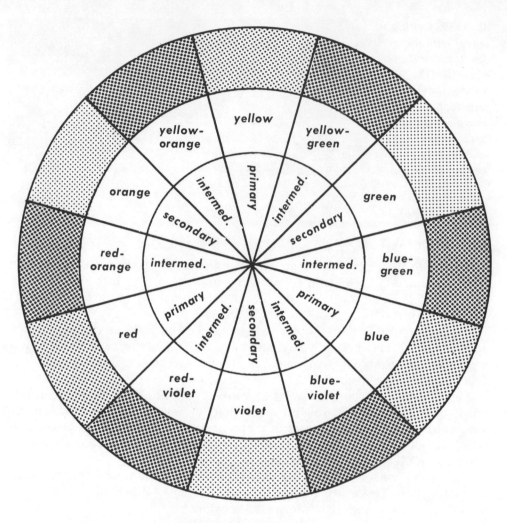

Illus. 18. The Color Wheel.

mentary colors." To "grey" a given color (dull it), mix in a more or less small quantity of its complementary color. By mixing complementary colors with varying amounts of white, an endless number of grey "tones" will result.

You can produce "tints" of color (lighter versions) by adding white; "shades" (darker versions) by adding black or sometimes burnt umber; and grey tones by adding a little black and white, or the complementary of the color plus white.

Measuring and Marking the Mat for Cutting

Placement of the Mat Opening

Should artwork ever occupy the exact center of the mat? You cannot say "never," but "hardly ever" is more like it. The two sides of the mat are always equal in width. The top may be the same or narrower or wider, while the bottom is a ½ in (12.7 mm) or so wider than the top. The amount of difference varies with the size of the mat: the bigger the mat, the greater the difference, all within reason, of course.

The reason for making the bottom of the mat wider is that a picture centered in the mat sometimes seems to "float" in the frame. This gives the viewer an uneasy feeling, as if fearing it is about to fall out. The wider bottom margin lends the arrangement something called "optical weight," pulling down on the picture and anchoring it in place. If the top and sides are 2 in (5.1 cm) wide, for instance, a 2½-in (6.4-mm) wide bottom is adequate. Making the bottom wider raises the center of the picture above the center of the mat and makes the bottom "look heavier." Your own judgment will be good enough here.

You will also have to depend on your own judgment in placing multiple windows in a mat, especially when the windows vary in size or shape, or if the photos or artwork differ in intensity of tone or color. The best way to decide on multiple placement is to lay out the art on a piece of matboard and move them around with respect to each other and the frame until they look right. Sketch what the final mat will look like and make exact measurements to be followed in cutting. Photographs are often matted without glass or mat, being dry-mounted directly on the mounting board.

Measuring the Mat for Cutting

Use a carpenter's square to determine whether or not the corners of the art are square. To find out if the opposite sides are parallel (as they must be), measure across the diagonals. If they are the same length, the

Illus. 19. A woodworker's marking gauge saves time and promotes accuracy in marking out the window opening on the back of the mat. The lines were inked in solely to make them show up in the photo. Don't bother to ink your lines.

art is square. How much it is out of square will determine how much to overlap the mat—⅛ in (3.2 mm) if the art is square.

All marking and cutting of the mat is done from the back. Pencil marks would show on the front and the face of the mat is easily damaged by scraping mat-cutting paraphernalia over it.

Measure the mat window opening and transfer the measurements to the back of the mat. Suppose you are mounting a picture cut from a magazine and it measures 5½ in (14 cm) wide by 7 in (17.8 cm) high. Cut the opening 5¼ in (13.3 cm) wide by 6¾ in (17.1 cm) high in an 8 × 10 in (20.3 × 25.4 cm) mat. The mat will be 1⅜ in (3.5 cm) wide on each side and the top can be the same, leaving 1⅝ in (4.2 cm) for the bottom width. If you use a woodworker's marking gauge (Illus. 19), you can draw the lines faster and be sure of your measurements.

Run your lines from edge to edge of the mat as shown, and you will never find yourself wondering where they are when the straightedge covers them.

Cutting the Mat

You may cut a mat with a single window opening, a double opening (Illus. 1), or with multiple openings. These can be square, rectangular, diamond-shaped, round-cornered, circular, oval or any other shape you desire. Mat-cutting is most easily done when you keep the shape of the window simple.

Illus. 20. Making a vertical cut with the mat knife against the vertical edge of a ⅜-in (9.5-mm)-thick straight-edge. The mat-cutting jig is clamped to the table.

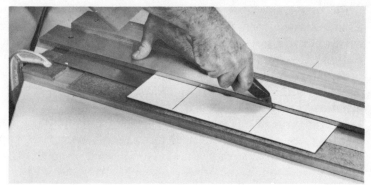

Illus. 21. The straightedge turned over to present its bev-elled edge to the knife. The blade is pressed flat against the sloping edge in making a bevel cut.

Illus. 22. The hand holding the knife does the cutting while the other hand lends support and rides rigidly on the face of the straightedge to assure maintain-ing the angle of the cut.

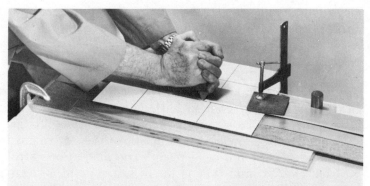

For most cuts, you need only a straightedge and a mat knife. If you want rounded corners, practice cutting a few on scrap matboard, using a woodworker's gouge, an arch punch or a hand-held circle cutter set to a radius of ¾ in to 1 in (19–25 mm). With practice, you can gain enough skill to cut round corners freehand with a mat knife.

Start with vertical cuts. Leave cutting bevels until after you have practiced on scrap matboard.

Matted artwork is almost always framed behind glass. Besides complementing the art, the practical purpose of the mat is to hold hinged art in place and to provide an air space between the art and the glass. The art must *never* touch the glass, not even if it is only a reproduction or a magazine cutout. Such contact can result in serious damage to the art from moisture condensation, staining and/or lifting of the ink. It also promotes the growth of mould. An original etching, framed before the ink is fully dry (which may take a while), will mark its pattern on the inner surface of the glass, even when separated from it by a mat. This necessitates demounting and cleaning the glass.

Before you do any serious mat-cutting, make some practice cuts to get the feel of the knife and the straightedge. (Illus. 20–22.) Don't cut directly on the base of the jig. Sufficient space has been left under the bar to allow passage of a piece of ⅛-in (3.2-mm) thick *untempered* hardboard or cardboard. Don't use corrugated cardboard.

Leave the hardboard underlay loose so it can be shifted after each cut. When it has become too scored for accurate cutting, replace it. Brookstone sells a 6′ (1.8 m) strip of zinc alloy for mat-cutting. It won't dull the point of the knife and lasts a long time. It saves money in the long run over the cost of hardboard. However, place hardboard under the zinc to protect the jig against slips.

Place a piece of hardboard on the jig, but don't clamp it down when you clamp the jig to the table. If you have a zinc cutting strip, place it on top and cover it with the mat and the straightedge. Line up one of the long cutting lines with the straightedge, give the knife blade a few strops on a razor strop or a piece of leather glued to a piece of wood, and sink the point vertically through the matboard, precisely in the corner where the lines cross (see Illus. 20 for the set-up for making a vertical cut). With the jig, you don't have to bear down so hard on the straightedge, so you can devote most of your attention to bearing down on the knife, not only downward but also sideways, against the straightedge.

Pull the knife toward you and make the entire cut in one smooth, even stroke. If you do not cut through the mat in one stroke, you will have to go back over it, and that is likely to result in a ragged cut that you may or may not be able to fix up with fine sandpaper (#220). Watch what you are doing and stop the cut when the blade is a hairbreadth past the near crossline (the knife blade is at an angle, so the point should be directly under the line). An over-run cut ruins the mat and you will have to start over.

Make the other long cut next, and then the two short cuts. When done, don't yank the mat out from under the straightedge. Lift the latter off and lay it aside, then pick up the mat and turn it over. All four corners may still be attached. Use a razor blade or an X-Acto knife to finish the cuts into the corners.

Cutting a Bevel

If you try to hold the straightedge freehand (without the jig) and make a bevel cut, you may be disappointed. After having cut a number of mats vertically, you can practice on cutting a bevel, and then you will be ready to cut a mat with a beveled window. A thick straightedge (3/8 in [9.5 mm] thick) offers an advantage as it provides a broad track of steel for the knife blade to ride on (Illus. 21).

Slip the marked mat under the straightedge, with the latter lying across the opening. Slant the knife handle over the straightedge so that the blade angles through the mat in the direction of the outer edge of the mat.

Remember that you are making a cut roughly 50 percent deeper than a vertical cut and therefore you are going to have to exert a force at least 50 percent greater on the knife. Strike the knife through at the exact corner, where the cross line intersects the cutting line. Pull the knife the length of the cut, cutting all the way through at one stroke. Keep the blade pressed firmly against the bevel of the straightedge. Finish cutting the opening and cut out the corners.

If you have only a thin straightedge like the one in Illus. 22, you will find it very difficult to maintain the same angle throughout the cut, as such a straightedge offers little to bear against. Do as shown in Illus. 22: Clamp the straightedge over the mat to hold everything solid and use both hands on the knife. One hand does the cutting while the other supports it and maintains the angle by running the little finger along the face of the straightedge as a guide.

Cutting a Round Mat

Illus. 23 shows a round mat—a circle cut in a rectangular matboard. It could also be cut with an outer circle so as to fit into a circular picture frame.

Illus. 23. Round mat covered with unbleached linen canvas. A secondary mat of 100 percent rag paper, not visible, is placed between the glued fabric and rag paper for protection of the art from the effect of acid. An extremely narrow top mat, painted with gold paint, eases the transition from the main mat into the narrow, black frame.

Circles up to 8½ in (21.6 cm) in diameter can be cut with the little circle cutter shown in Illus. 24, but it cuts only a vertical edge. If you want a bevelled edge, there are circle cutters that cut circles up to 20 in (50.8 cm), 30 in (76.2 cm), and 40 in (102 cm).

It's a good idea to draw the circle first with a pencil-compass. Set the center-pin of the cutter in the compass center and bear down to press the knife point through the board. The mat must be C-clamped to the table—in two places if it is a large one. Do not let the center-point jump out or the cut won't be smooth. Hold it firmly in place and make the cut in short increments, an inch or two (2.5–5 cm) at a time.

If you don't have a circle cutter, you can cut a round mat in the same

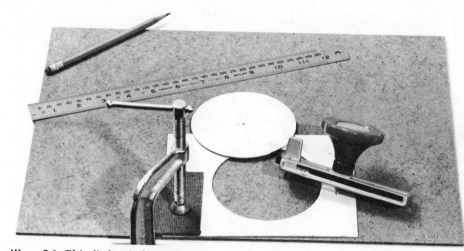

Illus. 24. This little circle cutter cuts vertical-edge rounds in matboard up to 8¼″ (21 cm) diameter. Cutting a circle is a two-handed operation, so always clamp the mat to the table.

way that will be described for cutting an oval window (see below), but, as in that case, the mat will have to be covered with paper or fabric to hide the uneven cut.

Drawing and Cutting an Ellipse for an Oval Mat

Practice first on paper, then transfer your effort to the back of the mat. The professional framer uses an oval-cutting machine, too expensive a device for the amateur craftsman.

With practice, you can learn to cut a passable oval or round window in a mat, using a mat knife freehand. In place of that, you can draw the figure on the back of the mat and cut it out with scissors (Illus. 25). First, however, you must learn how to draw an ellipse. This is done with a device called an "ellipsograph," and the simplest one consists of a couple of nails and a loop of thread (see Illus. 26–29). For a practice run, draw the major axis on a piece of paper and bisect it with the minor axis. Lay out on the axes the length and width of the oval—say, 5 × 7 in (12.7 × 17.8 cm). Mark the limits of the ellipse on both sides of the center.

In order to be able to construct an ellipse with your ellipsograph, you must first find the "foci," the two points into which you will drive the guiding nails. A law governing ellipses makes this simple. This law states that the distance from one focus to any point on the ellipse, plus the distance from that point to the other focus, is always equal to the length of the major axis (i.e., 7 in [17.8 cm] in this case).

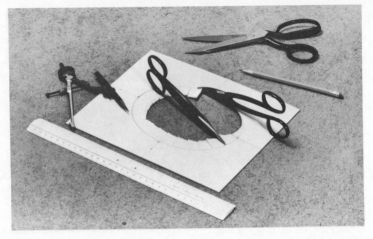

You need a compass to locate the foci. Set the compass to *one-half* the length of the major axis (make sure the pencil end is sharp) and set the point into the paper at either of the marks denoting the width on the minor axis. Strike an arc, crossing the major axis at two points (Illus. 26). These points are the foci.

Lay the paper on a piece of plywood and drive 6d (six-penny) finishing nails at the two foci and at the end of the major axis (Illus. 28). Tie a loop of linen or carpet thread (not string because it stretches) around the three nails and tie the two ends together in a hard knot at *A'*. Make it tight so it won't slip. Pull out the nail at *A'*. Its work is done.

Slip the point of a sharp pencil into the loop and pull it taut around the nails until the point rests at an end of the ellipse (Illus. 29). Now, keeping the loop taut, pull the pencil around the nails. Because the loop holds it in check and guides it, the point will describe the figure of an oval on the paper (Illus. 30).

When you can draw the ellipse without fumbling, you are ready to draw it directly on the back of the matboard.

◆ *Cutting Out An Elliptical Window.* As you will have to practice if you want to cut an oval freehand with a knife, you may want an oval mat before you master it, and here is how you can have one.

After drawing the ellipse on the mat, roughly cut the center out with scissors, to within about ½ in (12.7 mm) of the oval outline. The best tools for the job are jeweler's metal snips, one pair with straight blades and the other with curved. Go all around the ellipse with the straight shears, snipping in just to the line of the ellipse. Then take the curved snips and

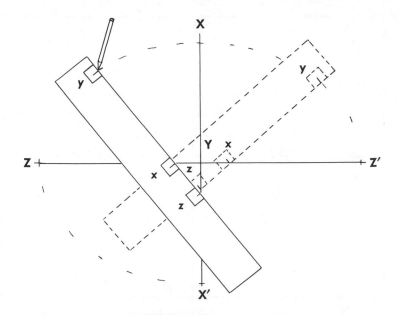

*Illus. 26. A laborious but accurate way to draw an el-
lipse, particularly a large one for constructing a frame, is
to use the same principle of measurement employed by
the modern ellipsograph. Draw the minor axis (X-X') and
the major axis (Z-Z') on a sheet of paper. On a ruler with
appropriately placed pieces of masking tape, or on a
strip of stiff paper, mark off the points equal to Y-X, or
one-half the minor axis, and Y-Z, or one-half the major
axis. Mark the points x, y and z as shown. With the point
x always riding on the Z-Z' axis and the point z always
riding on the X-X' axis, mark off the point y as many
times around the outline of the ellipse as necessary. Con-
nect the points with a solid line and cut out the ellipse.*

cut out the snipped tabs along the line. Both operations are shown in Illus.
31. If you don't have a circle cutter, you can cut out a circle the same way.

The result will be far from a smooth, even curve, even after you have
rubbed it down with a bone folder and touched it up where necessary with
garnet paper. However, you can hide such imperfections by covering the
mat with paper or fabric.

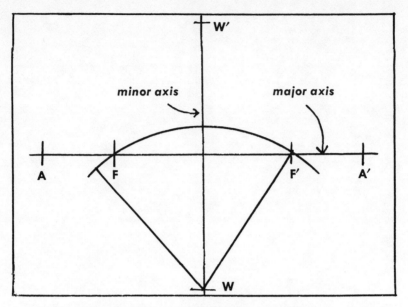

Illus. 27. First step in drawing an ellipse.

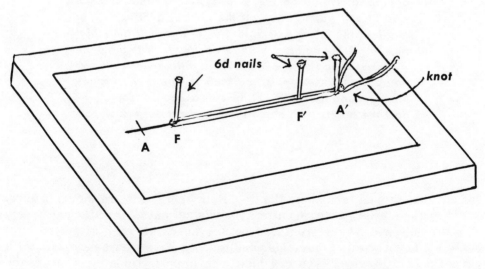

Illus. 28. Tying the loop of thread around the nails.

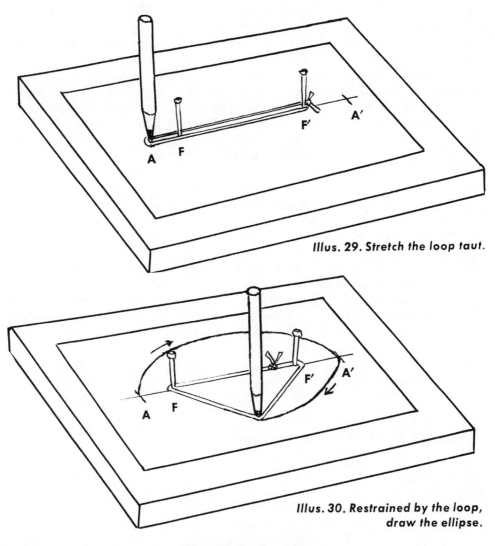

Illus. 29. Stretch the loop taut.

*Illus. 30. Restrained by the loop,
draw the ellipse.*

Covering the Mat

Covering a Rectangular Mat with Paper or Fabric

If you have "spoiled" a mat with a bad cut, you can save it by covering it with patterned or plain-colored paper. Cut a piece of the paper about 1 in (2.5 cm) larger all around than the mat and lay it face-down on a piece of waxed paper (glue won't stick to waxed paper).

The window may have either vertical or bevelled edges. With a vertical cut, gluing the edge of the board is taken care of by gluing the paper down on the back of the mat. If the window has bevelled edges, save the cutout and wipe each edge on coarse sandpaper a few times to make it one paper-thickness smaller.

Apply white glue, such as Record Brand Fabric Laminating Adhesive or Elmer's Glue-All, to the face side of the mat. Be sure to get glue on all the bevels. Lay the mat glued-side-down on the paper and press to adhere. Turn it over, place the cutout in the window and push it down. It should fit closely and present the same thickness as the rest of the mat as you roll it down with a hard rubber roller (Illus. 31).

Cover with waxed paper, a piece of hardboard and weight and leave it until the glue dries thoroughly—a couple of hours, or overnight to be safe. Then scissor off the excess paper around the edges, lay the mat face-down with the cutout in place and make two diagonal cuts with the mat knife through the paper in the window. Bend the resulting triangular tabs up-ward through the window, and cut off the tips (Illus. 32), leaving a tab 1 in (2.5 cm) or more wide along each side. Apply glue to the tabs (and to the edge of the window if it is a vertical cut), fold them over the back of the mat and rub them down. Cover with wax paper and press until the glue dries. While bending the tabs back, go over the edges of the window with a bone folder and rub them up to a clean, sharp edge while the glue is still wet and the paper flexible.

A second mat of heavy, 100 percent-rag paper or 2-ply museum board may be placed between the covered mat and the art to protect the latter from the glue. Heavy, 100 percent-rag watercolor paper is also excellent.

Covering a Round or Oval Mat with Paper

Illus. 25. Follow the procedure outlined above, but, since there are no real diagonals, cut two diameters perpendicular to each other through the paper in the window. Cut out the center to within about 1½ in (3.8 cm) of the outline. Snip these with scissors into narrow tabs about ⅜ in (9.5 mm) wide. Stop the snips ¹/₁₆ in (1.5 mm—the thickness of the mat) from the edge of the opening. Glue the tabs and fold them back over the edges of the window. Sharpen a vertical edge with the bone folder. Press until dry.

Covering Any Kind of Mat with Fabric

You can use any fabric you like, though it is wise to avoid very heavy fabrics since they will not fold well over the edges of the window. A fabric most commonly used is unbleached linen canvas (from an art supply

Illus. 31. When covering a bevel-cut mat with paper or fabric, the cut-out, made slightly smaller with sandpaper, is put back in place over the cover material. Press down against the glued bevel to assure its sticking. Then use a hard rubber roller over the material.

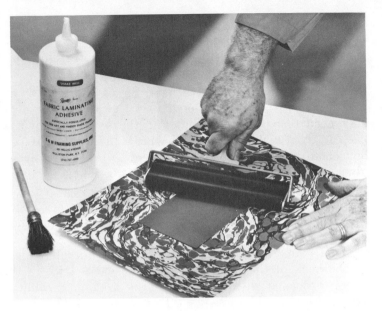

Illus. 32. Here is how the paper cover is cut into tabs and glued down on the back of the mat.

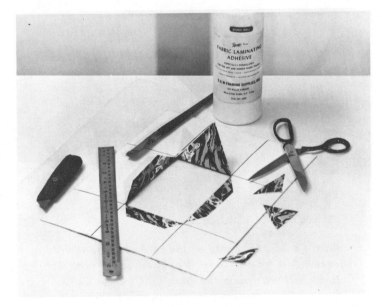

store). Less expensive, but attractive, is cotton Kasha cloth. Thin cotton, nylon or silk may also be used to cover a mat.

Use of a white polyvinyl acetate glue is especially important when covering with thin fabric because such a glue can be allowed to dry and then can be reactivated with heat. So all you have to do is paint the face of the mat with glue and let it dry. Lay the fabric over it. A thin fabric may need to be stretched out and thumbtacked down around the mat to keep it from wrinkling. Cover with a piece of Kraft paper and, with the household iron set a little above "low," proceed to iron the cloth into the glue (Illus. 33). Check to make sure the fabric adheres all over, then put it aside to cool under a board and weight.

By working this way, you won't have to worry about the glue seeping through the fabric and ruining the work. Examine the mat later for any loose spots and iron down any you may find.

Some framers turn the fabric over the outside edges and glue it down on the back of the mat, but this adds extra bulk in the rabbet, creating fitting problems with a frame having a shallow rabbet. You can trim off the excess with scissors—as with paper—or fold it over and glue it down, as you please.

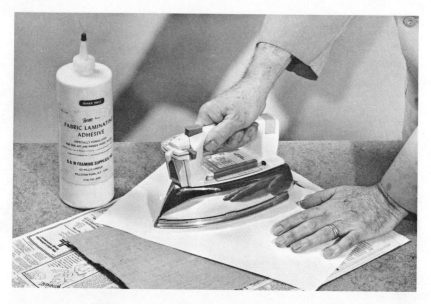

Illus. 33. To avoid glue on the face of the mat striking through a fabric cover, first let the glue dry. Then cover with fabric and iron it on. Heat will reacitvate the glue and make the bond. Use low heat on the iron.

Next, cut tabs in the window (Illus. 34) and glue them down to the back of the mat. Make sure the fabric adheres well to the edges. When the glue is dry, assemble the mat, mount the art, and the work is ready for framing. One of the mats being worked up in the illustrations is shown framed in Illus. 53.

You can help render the fabric resistant to dirt and stains by spraying with a fabric protector.

Other Mat Effects

You are not limited to covering the mat with paper or fabric in your search for unique effects. You may also resort to painting the mat with watercolors or acrylics thinned with water. Use white museum board, flow the colors on and brush them into attractive patterns.

Also, you can coat the mat with dark grey (or colored) gesso thinned with ⅓-part water. Add black to make grey. When it is dry, brush on a coat of thick acrylic gesso as it comes from the can. Let it set (thicken) a little, then take a broken piece of comb and rake through it, making vertical or horizontal furrows (or waves or swirls) that expose the grey gesso underneath. A colored gesso undercoat also produces nice results. When the gesso is dry and set hard, paint it with acrylic colors and highlight it with strokes of gilt or silver paint as described for finishing frames in Chapter 5.

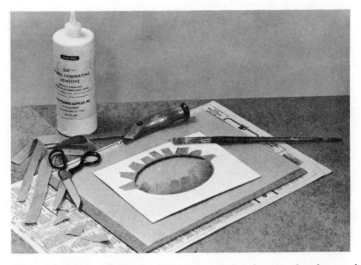

Illus. 34. Back of the oval mat reveals shape of tabs and how they look when they're glued down.

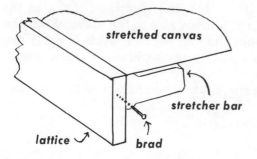

Illus. 35. Strip frame.

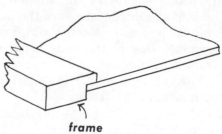

*Illus. 36. Painting on hardboard
or canvas board.*

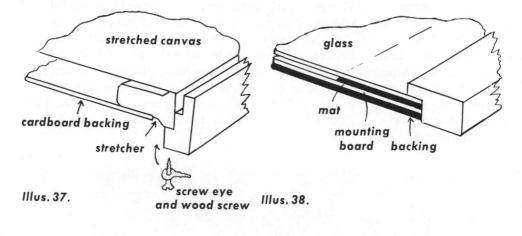

Illus. 37.

Illus. 38.

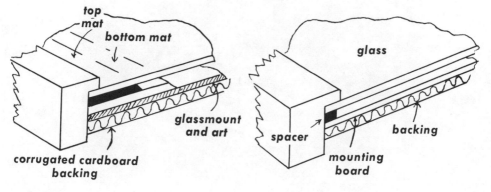

Illus. 39.

Illus. 40.

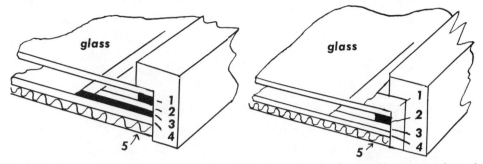

Illus. 41. A mount for fine art. 1) Spacer, 2) velvet-covered mat, 3) museum board, 4) backing.

Illus. 42. Matted art in frame with a fillet. 1) Fillet, 2) spacer, 3) mat, 4) mounting board, 5) backing.

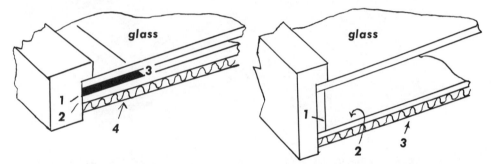

Illus. 43. Fitting for fine art, with glass sealed in. 1 and 2) Museum board mat and mounting board, 3) sheet of aluminum foil, 4) backing of corrugated cardboard.

Illus. 44. Box frame. 1) Box of lattice moulding, as deep as required by the objet d'art, 2) mounting board, 3) backing.

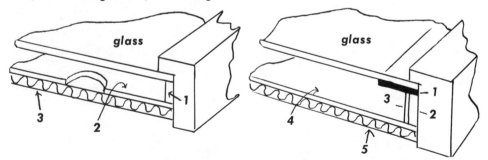

Illus. 45. Box frame for coin display. 1) Narrow lattice for shallow box, 2) mounting board holed for coins, 3) backing.

Illus. 46. Lined box frame. 1) Narrow mat, 2) lattice box, 3) matboard or fabric lining, 4) mounting board, 5) backing.

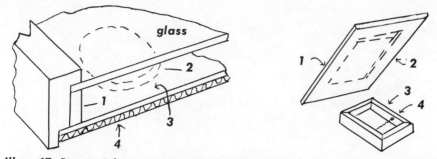

Illus. 47. Stepped frame. 1) Matboard glued to side of rabbet, 2) 3-dimensional art object, 3) mounting board, 4) backing.

Illus. 48. Panel mount. 1) Bleed photo or art pasted on panel, 2) hardboard panel, 3) box frame for flat-to-wall hanging, 4) wire.

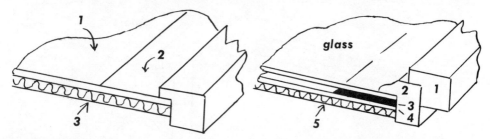

Illus. 49. Glassless framing of a photo. 1) Dry mounted photo, 2) mounting board, 3) backing (if needed).

Illus. 50. Frame with narrow insert or fillet. 1) Frame, 2) insert, 3) mat, 4) mounting board, 5) backing.

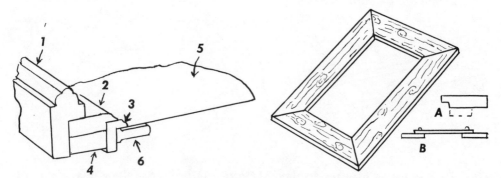

Illus. 51. 1 Frame, 2) insert, 3) fillet, 4) filler strip, 5) stretched canvas, 6) stretcher bar.

Illus. 52. Flat frame, A) with rabbet, B) with overlapping mount.

44

Illus. 53. Mounted and framed, the old mine building seems in its element, surrounded by a marbled pattern of browns and greys reminiscent of stone.

**Cutting
and Fitting
the Glass**

Cutting Glass for the Picture Frame

Preliminaries and Tools

Even if you intend to frame pictures only as a hobby, you should know something about cutting glass and even do the work yourself, especially if you like to master all the techniques of a project.

Oil and acrylic paintings are not glassed because the artist has already protected the painted surface with one or more coats of picture varnish. Varnishing pictures is a matter for the restorer and need not concern you.

However, if you have only a few frames to glaze, it will not pay for you to cut your own glass. Instead, you can buy single-strength window glass (about .08 in or 5/64 in thick—about 2 mm) at a hardware store, and cutting is included in the price. Picture glass, however, can be purchased only at a place that deals exclusively in glass. It is also called 14-oz glass and is less than $\frac{1}{16}$ in (1.5 mm) thick; it is therefore lighter in weight than window glass. At a glass house, you can get picture glass cut to any reasonable shape—rectangular, round or oval. In the last two cases, take the frame along to be sure the glass will fit.

On the other hand, the dyed-in-the-wool do-it-yourselfer will want to cut his own glass. There is a trick to cutting it, but anybody can quickly learn. You don't need much equipment—a glass-cutter, a straightedge and a piece of carpet or cardboard on which to do the cutting.

Glass is sold in panes or sheets by glass firms. A standard size is 24 × 30 in (61 × 76 cm). The glass-cutter does its work either with a steel or carbide wheel or with a point of industrial diamond. Carbide outlasts steel and diamond outlasts both. The latter is more costly, but it makes a better score with less pressure. Sometimes the wheel-type is fitted with a large carrier wheel holding a half-dozen cutting wheels. When a wheel wears out, loosen the center screw, position a new wheel and tighten the screw.

The notches in the handle of some cutters are sized to fit various thicknesses of glass and are used to break off small bits that may cling to the score-line. Glass-breaking pliers (Illus. 54) are better for the job, though.

Before each use, the wheel glass-cutter must be dipped in paint thinner, but the diamond is used dry and is therefore more convenient.

Another type is the combination glass-cutter and glass-plier. The upper jaw is so shaped that when the lower is placed under the score line and the handles squeezed together, the upper jaw exerts equal pressure against the glass on each side of the line, thereby breaking it.

Illus. 54. Start the glass cutter at the far edge of the glass, not overhanging it. Diamond cutter shown. Glass pliers in foreground are used to break off bits of glass clinging to the score should the cut go crooked.

Before doing any serious glass-cutting, experiment on scrap. Ask for scrap where you buy your glass and practice with it. It takes a few tries before you catch on to just how much pressure to apply.

Cutting the Glass

Don't cut glass directly on the hard table surface. Lay a piece of cardboard down, or a piece of short-napped rug such as professionals use.

An aluminum rule makes a good straightedge. It should have a nonslip pad on the bottom, or shoe it with pieces of masking tape to provide a nonskid surface. Mark the glass with a soft-tip marking pen and line up the straightedge with the marks, but as far inside the measurement as the space between the guiding edge of the cutter and the cutting point or wheel, usually about $\frac{1}{16}$ in (1.5 mm).

Remember that the glass must have the same dimensions as the mat—$\frac{1}{8}$ in (3.2 mm) less in length and width than the rabbet opening in the frame. A tight-fitting glass easily gets broken.

See Illus. 54 for starting the cut. The cutter is *at* the edge, not in front of it nor overhanging it. With a diamond cutter, the overhang could cause the diamond to be pulled out. Bear down firmly and draw the cutter toward you with a swift, smooth motion, directly to the near edge of the glass. Keep the wrist and fingers stiff and make the move with shoulder and elbow. You will hear a steady continuous sound of crushing glass as the cutter moves across the glass.

If the sound stutters, your line will have skips and jumps in it and the glass will not break true. That is why you need to practice before making a cut in expensive glass.

The score shows white against the glass (Illus. 55) and should be of the same intensity from one end to the other.

Breaking the Scored Glass

The easiest way to break the scored glass is to hold it in your hands (Illus. 55) and twist your hands away from each other, as if you were breaking a twig. The glass should break cleanly all along the score. If it doesn't, it is a sign that it was not correctly scored and you will have to try again.

There are other ways to break the glass. You can lay a pencil or a dowel under the score and bend the glass over it until it breaks. Another way is to use the combination cutter-plier. Still another is to lay the glass on the table, the waste hanging over the table edge and the score lined up with it. Hold the glass down on the table side and press down on the

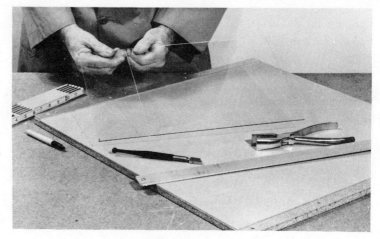

Illus. 55. Break glass between your hands as you would break a twig. The cutting jig shown is a commercial job that is a help in speeding up accurate cutting.

free side until the glass breaks along the score. Wear leather-palmed work gloves to guard against injury.

Also, always wear eye proection when cutting glass. Tiny fragments shoot out from the cutter and litter the table. Keep the area covered with newspapers that can be gathered up and disposed of after cutting is done. If bits of glass fall outside the paper-covered area, don't risk picking them up with your fingers. Keep some modelling clay handy, the kind that never dries out. Take a small piece and use it to pick up stray particles. Discard the clay along with the glass.

Cutting Glass for a Round Frame

Cutting a circle in glass needs a special circle cutter made for that purpose, as the cut must be made with uniform pressure and in a single, circular sweep, a feat that takes some practice.

Cut a square piece of glass an inch or two (2.5–5.1 cm) larger than the diameter of the desired circle. Draw diagonals on a piece of cardboard and use it for an underlay (Illus. 56). This will help you locate the center for the suction cup of the circle cutter. First, take a piece of cotton or a tissue dipped in paint thinner and wrap it around the cutter part. Without touching the cutting wheel to the glass, swing the cutter around in a full circle, cleaning the glass with the paint thinner and preparing the surface for cutting.

As shown in Illus. 56, your point of departure is with arms crossed and the cutter brought back as far as possible toward yourself. Turn down the

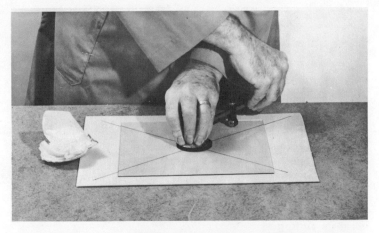

Illus. 56. Cardboard with marked diagonals locates center of glass for cutter and serves as an underlay. Start in the position shown so that you can make the complete turn without hesitating or stopping to shift your grip.

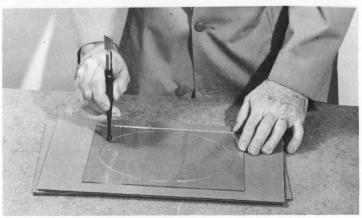

Illus. 57. Turn the glass scored-side down on corrugated cardboard and tap around the score to break it.

Illus. 58. Next score radial lines, starting ⅜" (9.5 mm) circle to edge of glass. Experts do this freehand. A straightedge helps the beginner keep the scores straight.

lever on the center column. This draws the air out of the suction cup. Hold the center of the device down firmly with one hand and apply pressure to the cutter with the other. Quickly swing the cutter around and back to its starting position. If you did it right, you will have an even score all around, with no skips or weak spots.

Put the cutter aside and turn the glass over on corrugated cardboard (Illus. 57) so that the scored circle is on the bottom. Take the straight glass-cutter and tap around the circle with the end of its handle. The glass breaks along the score as you progress.

Next, turn the glass over and make a series of radial scores, starting about ⅜ in (9.5 mm) from the circle and out to the edge of the glass (Illus. 58). Make them as shown in the photograph and use a straightedge to guide the cutter.

Turn the glass over again so that the radial scores are on the bottom and tap over each with the glass-cutter until you see the score-line break. As you work your way around the square, the glass enclosing the circle breaks free. Break off any protruding points with glass pliers and remove sharp edges with a sharpening stone dipped in water.

Fitting

Getting everything together in proper order for framing is called fitting, because the contents are being fitted into the frame. The glass is generally just eased into place, followed by the mat and the other components. However, if it is a case of preserving valuable artwork, you should first paint the rabbet of the frame with a couple of coats of matte acrylic medium. Wood is quite acidic and the medium will seal it away from the artwork.

Sealing the Glass

Not in every case, but in some, the glass is sealed into place to prevent the incursion of air, dust, moisture and or insects. Space the glass so that its edges are equidistant from the sides of the rabbet all around. Then take a strip of masking tape the length of one long side and stick it down to the edge of the glass. With a table knife, poke the tape down between the glass and the side of the rabbet and rub it down on the wood. Do the same to the other long side and then to both short sides. Make sure that the tape does not extend far enough over the glass to be visible beyond the lip of the rabbet from the outside.

Next add the 100-percent-rag museum board mat and mounting board and a backing board of the same or of foam-cored board, or a piece of 8-ply museum board.

If the glass is sealed in a box-type frame, it should be held in firmly with glazing points after sealing.

If corrugated cardboard is used for backing, line the inside face with a sheet of heavy-duty aluminum foil to prevent the passage of acidic atmosphere through the mounting board.

Fitting with Brads

Five-eighth-inch (16-mm) brads are most often used to hold the package in the frame. Care must be taken, particularly with a light frame, not to knock the frame apart when driving in the brads.

A magnetic brad pusher is one way of driving the brads into the side of the frame (Illus. 59). Another way is to hammer them in with a fitting hammer. This is a professional tool with a specially shaped head, but any small hammer will do. Let the head rub on the backing as you strike the brad. Brace the side of the frame against a board clamped to the table to absorb the shock.

The fitting tool (Illus. 61) puts no strain on any part of the frame. The vertical force of squeezing the handles together is translated into a horizontal force, causing the end jaw to push the brad into the frame. The jaw outside the frame is padded to avoid marring the finish.

Fitting with a Point Driver

The point driver is a glazier's tool that is used to drive diamond-shaped zinc points into a window frame to hold the glass in before puttying. The #2 size point is preferred for framing. If you use this machine, be sure to brace the frame against a clamped board, as the spring lets go with considerable force. The point driver provides the fastest way of doing the final fitting job.

Sealing the Back

Only glassed frames should be sealed at the back to prevent entry of dust, grease, moisture and insects. The common practice of stripping over the crack between the backing and the frame with gummed-paper tape is not recommended. Although the gummed tape sticks quite well to the wood of the frame, in a short time it loses its hold on the backing material and opens up the back. The worst is, you won't know it unless you examine the back closely.

The best method is to cut a piece of Kraft paper slightly smaller than the size of the frame at the back. Brush Elmer's Glue-All or a similar glue in a path around the back of the frame. Don't leave any spaces. Dampen

Illus. 59. The frame can be fitted with ⅝-" (16-mm) brads, using a brad pusher. Keep pliers handy to pull out any mis-drives.

Illus. 60. The fitting hammer is a professional tool. Shape of head lets hammer lie flat with handle elevated. C-clamp a board to table to take driving force, prevent damaging frame.

Illus. 61. The fitting tool comes with short or long jaws. Long shown. When you squeeze handles, inside jaw approaches frame, driving brad into wood. Padded outside jaw won't mar a finished frame.

the paper with a sponge, lay it over the back of the frame and rub it down over the glued strip. The dampness will cause the paper to stretch a little. As it dries, it shrinks. At the same time, the glue takes hold and, when both glue and paper are dry, the seal is stretched drum-tight across the back.

If the paper should get torn or punctured, the seal is no longer effective, but it can be corrected simply by pasting a piece of paper over the damaged area.

Remember, though, that all your sealing efforts will be in vain if the materials in the frame are not of 100-percent-rag constitution. The only exception is the final backing, and only if it is separated from the materials inside with aluminum foil.

Paintings on Stretched Canvas

As mentioned before, an oil or acrylic painting is not mounted under glass (except in exceptional circumstances of an old work of art or unusual ambient conditions). Moreover, the back is never sealed, since the canvas must have access to a free circulation of air.

When such a painting is taken down from the wall, it sometimes happens that its back is thoughtlessly placed against a table corner or some other sharp point, making work for the restorer. To avoid this, the back should be covered with cardboard stapled to the stetcher-bars all around. Before mounting it, however, cut a 1-in (2.5-cm) hole in each corner to allow air to circulate between the cardboard and the canvas. If the painting is fairly large, one or two similar holes in addition, on the centerline near the middle of the canvas, will assure adequate ventilation.

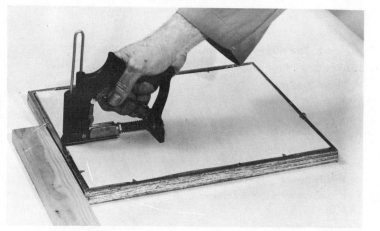

Illus. 62. The point driver is a glazier's tool, favored by framers. Spring-drive forces #2 diamond-shaped zinc glazing point into wood. Brace frame against a clamped-down stop.

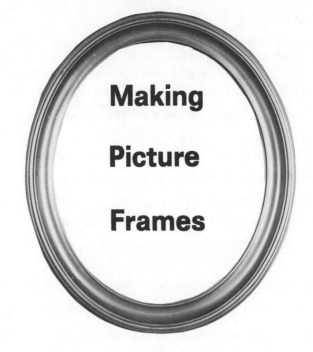

Making

Picture

Frames

Making Your Own Picture Frame Mouldings

This book encourages you to try to make your own frames from "scratch." If you would rather buy your frames ready-made but unfinished, you can impress your own personality on them by carving some simple design around the edge (Illus. 80). Carving and finishing will be further treated in the next chapter.

Check a ready-made frame closely before purchasing and pick out the best one in the desired size. Smooth with fine sandpaper to get rid of any inequalities at the mitres and any rough places.

You can also buy unfinished picture-frame moulding at some lumber-yards and variety stores. You can cut your own mitres and custom-fit the frame to the art you want to frame.

Tools and Materials

♦ *Wax Crayons.* (Illus. 63–64). For filling nail holes and covering blemishes in prefinished frames or picture-frame moulding. Take a little on the point of a pocketknife and press it into nail holes, selecting a color of crayon that matches the color of the frame.

♦ *Wood Filler.* For filling nail holes in unpainted frames.

♦ *Glue.* Brookstone's Speed Set Glue, Elmer's Carpenter's Glue, Weldbond, or use a two-component glue such as 5-minute epoxy.

♦ *Rasps with Replaceable Blades.* Purchase at your hardware store.

♦ *Files and Rifflers.* Round files in sizes up to ¾ in (19 mm), flat files, half-rounds, grit-files, rifflers such as sculptors use, etc.

♦ *Carving Tools.* Carving tools are available in small sets, or buy a ½-in (12.7-mm) gouge, and chisels in a couple of sizes.

♦ *Combination Square.* For squaring, measuring and marking.

♦ *Corner Clamps.* You need four. Used in assembling frames.

♦ *Other Clamps.* Spring clamps, C-clamps, adjustable clamps—all have dozens of uses around the framing shop. If spring clamps are not provided with plastic-covered jaws, pad them with cardboard and masking tape to keep clamps from marring the wood.

♦ *Block Plane.* For planing outer edges of frames into round edges.

♦ *Pliers.* For pulling out bent nails.

♦ *Hand Drill.* Use brad as a bit and drill holes in corners of the frame for nailing mitres together after gluing (see Illus. 65).

♦ *Diagonal Wirecutters.* For pulling out brads sunk too deep to be pulled with pliers, and for cutting picture wire.

♦ *Hammers.* A 6-oz brad hammer and a 10-oz claw hammer.

♦ *Stapler.* Hand or electric. Use ⅜-in (9.5-mm) staples for stapling cardboard to stretcher-frames, ⁹⁄₁₆-in (13.5-mm) across mitre joints at back.

♦ *Awl.* For marking, making starting holes for drill.

♦ *Nail Set.* With ¹⁄₃₂-in (1-mm) tip.

♦ *Locking Pliers.* Break old bandsaw and hacksaw blades into short lengths. Grip with pliers and use to "distress" surface in antiquing.

Illus. 63. Some tools for frame-making. 1) Wood filler and crayons for filling nail holes, and so on. 2) Stapler with ⅜-" (9.5-mm) and ⁹⁄₁₆-" (14.3-mm) staples. 3) Glue. 4) Corner clamp, need four. 5) Combination square. 6) Round and flat rasps. 7) Awl, nail set, pliers. 8) Block plane. 9) Hand drill. 10) Spring clamps. 11) C-clamps. 12) Locking plier with bits of bandsaw and hacksaw blade for distressing frames. 13) Round rasp. 14) Narrow flat rasp. 15) Wide flat rasp. 16) 5-oz and 10-oz hammers.

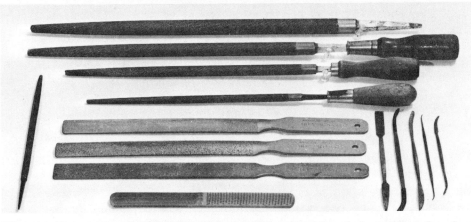

Illus. 64. Here are round files, flat files, grit files, a rasp and some rifflers for shaping and carving frames by hand.

Illus. 65. The frame-making jig with frame members in place for joining. Hand drill drills corners for bradding. Brads hold mitres when frame is turned to join other side.

◆ *The Mitre Box.* The framer's most important tool. The cheapest are made of wood or plastic and will do until they wear out. A better one is shown in Illus. 66; it is relatively inexpensive and suitable for mitring light moulding. A medium-priced mitre box (Illus. 67) performs better and lasts indefinitely. It can be adjusted to cut any angle in increments of ¼ or ½ degree. Get one with a 26-in (66-cm) saw with a 4-in (10.2-cm) depth of cut, or a 28-in (71-cm) saw with a 5-in (12.7-cm) depth of cut.

◆ *The Picture-frame Jig.* A complete frame-making shop for the amateur. Use to mitre frame members, then to assemble the frame (Illus. 65).

◆ *The Chopsaw.* An electric mitre saw (Illus. 68). The 10-in (25.4-cm), high-speed (5500 rpm) blade and precision construction assure smooth, highly accurate mitre joints. A fine tool for the home craftsman with a woodworking shop, but rather expensive for the occasional framer. Take safety precautions and wear eye protection when using this or any other power tool.

Illus. 66. An inexpensive mitre box with a 16" mitre saw, a reasonably priced item that will cut accurate mitres.

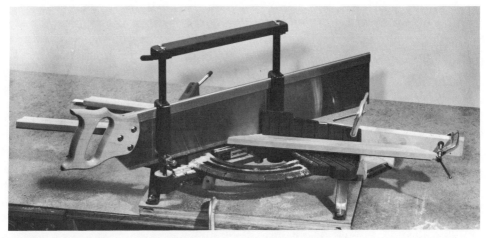

Illus. 67. A medium-priced mitre box with a 26-" (66-cm) mitre saw that cuts to a depth of 4" (10.2 cm). Adjustable to saw at any angle, left or right. When not in use, saw hangs at top of frame, lets you use both hands when placing mould-ing for cutting. Note C-clamp used as a stop at right to assure equal length of opposite frame members. Saw mitres mouldings to 6" (15.2 cm) wide by 4" (10.2 cm) deep.

Illus. 68. The electric mitre saw or chopsaw. For high-speed production with great accuracy. High-speed blade (5500 rpm) mitres moulding to 2⁷⁄₁₆″ (61.9 mm) high by 3¾″ (9.5 cm) wide.

Using the Mitring Equipment

A mitre box consists of a bed to which the moulding is clamped, either with a clamp that is part of the mitre box or with a C-clamp; a fence to hold the moulding correctly with respect to the angle of the saw; and the saw frame, which can be set to either side of center to cut mitres for every kind of polygonal figure. A good mitre box has an arrangement for suspending the saw at the top of the guides, so that it is out of the way and you can use both hands in placing the moulding.

First, for easy handling, cut your moulding with square ends to a length equalling that of one long member plus one short member, plus 2 in (5.1 cm) or 3 in (7.6 cm) over for good measure. You will have two pieces of moulding for one frame.

You can make your first mitre cut to either side of the zero mark. Suppose you set the saw for the first cut at 45° to the right of center. Clamp the moulding and make the first mitre cut (Illus. 69). Clamp the second piece of moulding and mitre the end.

The second cut is made with the saw to the left of center (Illus. 70). Study Illus. 71. Use the information in it to calculate the length of the two long frame members and mark this measurement on the outside edge of the frame stick. It makes no difference whether you cut the moulding with the rabbet edge or the outside edge against the fence. Just make sure the piece ends up shorter on the rabbet side.

Swing the saw 45° to left of center and lock it. Adjust the moulding so that the mark you made just touches the sawteeth, and clamp the moulding in place.

Illus. 69. Illustrating the first or right-hand cut with the mitre box. Note how moulding is clamped to the bed and held in against the fence. Moulding is being cut with rabbet edge away from fence.

Illus. 70. The second cut of a frame member is made with saw handle swung to the left. Note clamping and stop block to assure cutting opposite frame members to the same length.

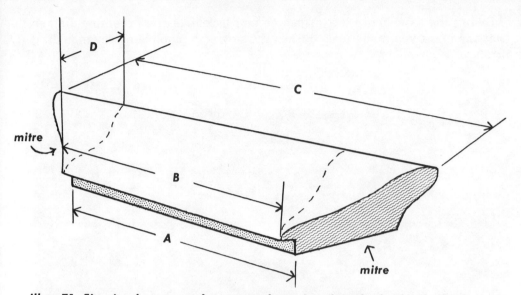

Illus. 71. Figuring how to cut frame members. A = length of side of rabbet = art or mat dimension plus ⅛″ (3.2 mm). B = length of rabbet lip or frame opening = A minus ½″ (12.7 mm); or, minus 2× the width of the rabbet. C = outside measure from tip to tip of the mitres = B + 2D, where D = overall width of moulding.

It is better to mark measurements on the outside edge of the frame piece, rather than on the side of the rabbet, for it is the only place where you can place the work against the saw for positioning.

Note, in Illus. 67 and 70, how a stop-block is fixed so as to contact the outboard tip of the mitre. If your mitre box does not have a stop-gauge built into it, jury-rig or improvise one by clamping a piece of 1 × 2 to the back of the fence. Clamp a stop-block to the 1 × 2, just touching the tip of the mitre, or simply use a C-clamp for a stop.

Saw the mitre and remove the moulding. Place the second moulding with the mitre tip against the stop; clamp and saw. This way you can be absolutely certain that opposite frame members are identical in length (otherwise your frame will be lopsided). Cut the second pair of frame members the same way.

Lumberyard Mouldings

(Illus. 72A and B.)

These are mouldings used by builders in the construction of homes and buildings. You may find them in pine, fir, redwood or some other softwood, depending on your locale. You will not find a complete line at any lumber-yard, so you will probably need to visit several to find what you want.

Lumberyard mouldings are not intended for picture-framing and there-fore lack a rabbet. You will have to provide one by gluing a strip of lattice or parting stop to the back, set in to leave a rabbet about $\frac{5}{16}$ in (7.5 mm) wide. Some mouldings have a hollow back which you will have to fill in order to glue a piece on. A narrow strip of matboard or cardboard can be glued in the hollow and the rabbet strip glued on over it (Illus. 73).

Don't confuse "picture moulding" with "picture-frame moulding." Picture moulding was used in old-fashioned, high-ceilinged homes to separate the wallpaper from the ceiling paper, which was brought down 1 ft (30 cm) or so on the walls to make the ceiling appear lower. Pictures were suspended from the moulding on long, fabric-covered wires—hence the name. As for joining or assembling the frame, observe Illus. 65. It shows how the frame-making jig, after you have used it to saw the mitres, is used to assemble or join the frame. Note the hand drill used to drill holes for the brads that hold the mitres together until the glue sets. For more details, see Chapter 5.

Making Your Own Picture-Frame Moulding

The tools you need to make your own picture-frame mouldings consist of a radial-arm or bench saw and/or a router. With these tools you do not have to depend on the availability of mouldings, but you can make your own.

Fir, pine, redwood, cedar, hemlock and other softwoods (depending on what part of the country you live in) are commonly available in standard lumber sizes such as 1×2, 1×3, 1×4 and so on. These sizes are the *rough* lumber only. *Planed* lumber so designated measures $\frac{3}{4} \times 1\frac{1}{2}$ in (1.9 $\times$ 3.8 cm), $\frac{3}{4} \times 2\frac{1}{2}$ in (1.9 $\times$ 6.4 cm), $\frac{3}{4} \times 3\frac{1}{2}$ in (1.9 $\times$ 8.9 cm) and so on. Philippine mahogany and hardwoods generally still adhere to the old-fashioned measurements of $1\frac{3}{16}$ in (20.6 mm) thick, while widths run to $\frac{5}{8}$-in (16-mm) increments. Take a tape measure with you when you go to buy lumber and determine first-hand what the standard dimensions are for your locality. Always buy first-quality lumber and take your time picking it out, to get pieces without knots or twisted grain.

You may find pine the easiest wood to work with. Whatever wood you choose, buy the narrowest width your moulding requires. The narrower the board, the lower the per-board-foot cost. Wide boards cost more per board-foot and do not represent a saving when bought in quantity.

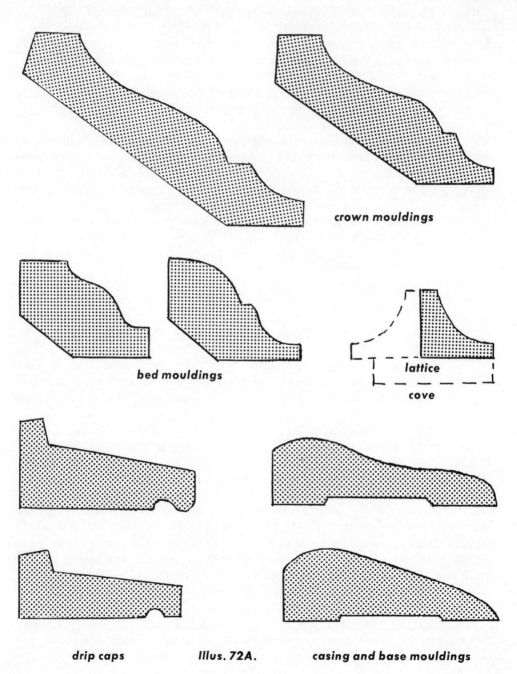

crown mouldings

bed mouldings

lattice

cove

drip caps

Illus. 72A.

casing and base mouldings

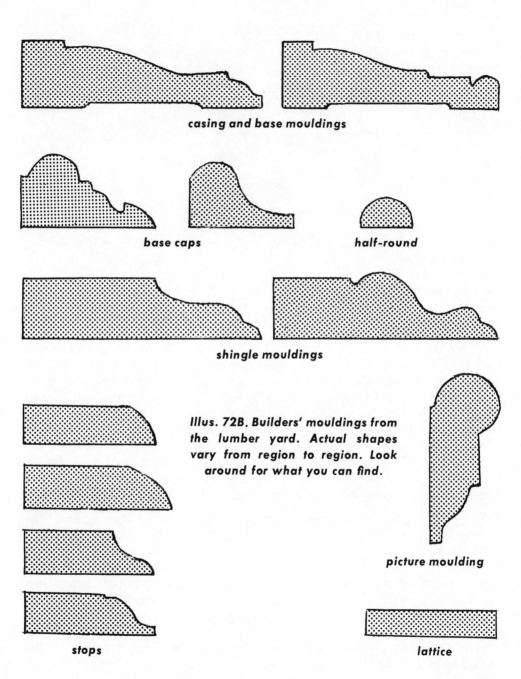

casing and base mouldings

base caps

half-round

shingle mouldings

Illus. 72B. Builders' mouldings from the lumber yard. Actual shapes vary from region to region. Look around for what you can find.

stops

picture moulding

lattice

Illus. 73. Lumber-yard mouldings glued into picture-frame moulding. Foreground: ¾" (19.1 mm) half-round and ½" (12.7 mm) × ¾" (19.1 mm) parting stop. Background: 2¼" (5.7 cm) detail moulding and 1⁵⁄₁₆" (3.3 cm) × ¼" (6.4 mm) lattice to form a rabbet. Nailed or clamped together. Note jaw protection on clamps.

Moulding and Shaping

Moulding is working the surface of a board with a moulding head and cutters. Shaping is done on the edge of the board. The router shapes and sometimes moulds; the moulding head moulds and sometimes shapes. In moulding with the radial-arm saw, the work is fed under the cutters and against their revolution. With the bench saw, the cutters work from beneath and the piece is always fed from the front of the saw table.

You can handle the work more easily if you divide a frame between two workpieces, each consisting of a long side and a short side of the prospective frame, plus 6 in (15.2 cm) or 8 in (20.3 cm) over to take care of the end-sniping that almost always occurs at the trailing end of the board.

◆ *The Router.* Narrow frames are most easily made by shaping the edge of a wide board with the router (Illus. 74–75). The edge can also be shaped with the router fixed in a router table (Illus. 76). When using the router freehand on a straight board, make the cut from left to right. Illus. 77–78 show how to complete the moulding by rabbeting with a dado head, then cutting the moulding off the board. A wide frame that provides a surface for the base of the router can be routed after assembly. Do it in several passes.

Illus. 79 shows how to mitre a box-frame member simply by tilting the sawblade to a 45° angle.

66

Illus. 74. A 1 h.p. router is a companion to the radial arm saw for making mouldings. For narrow mouldings, the router shapes the edge of a wider board. The saw then cuts the rabbet and cuts the moulding off the board.

Illus. 75. When the router bit has no pilot, an edge guide is mounted to keep the cutter moving in a straight line. It can make surface cuts this way as well as edge cuts.

Illus. 76. The router table turns the router into a shaper. Note the auxiliary wood table and the wood springs for holding the work against the fence.

Illus. 77. After you have shaped the edge of a board with the router to make a narrow frame, plow the rabbet groove with a dado head in the saw. Wood springs hold the work in place as you push it through, and prevent sideways creeping.

Illus. 78. After the rabbet has been grooved out of the board, cut the moulding off with a regular combination saw blade.

Illus. 79. When mitre-sawing lattice for a box frame, or for any flat moulding that is higher than it is wide, saw the mitre with the saw blade set at a 45° angle. See profiles 32, 33 and 34.

Making a Simple Moulding

Start with an easy profile—select one of those from 1 to 20. Always use hold-downs and wood springs (Illus. 77) when shaping with the router table or moulding with the saw. Side or vertical play cannot be tolerated as this results in unusable moulding. When using the router freehand, nail or clamp back- and end-stops to the work table against which the board will press to avoid chattering or slipping. You can even nail the workpiece to the table with a 1¼-in (3.2-cm) brad at each end in a place where it will not contact the revolving router bit.

If the router bit has no pilot (Illus. 81) or guide, use a router table (Illus. 76), or use an edge guide on the router (Illus. 75). Many cuts can also be made with a shaper if you are fortunate enough to own one.

After shaping the profile, plow the rabbet (Illus. 77), then cut the moulding off the board. The groove may be dadoed ¼ in to ⁵⁄₁₆ in (6.4–8 mm) deep to form the width of the rabbet. The width of the dado you use depends on how much room you will need in the rabbet for glass, mat and backing—³⁄₈ in (9.5 mm) or more.

The rabbet for an oil or acrylic painting on stretched canvas is best made as deep as the thickness of the stretcher-bars plus the canvas at front and back—a little over ¾ in (19 mm), say, ¹³⁄₁₆ in (20.6 mm), the maximum width the dado will cut in a single pass, though the rabbet may also be shallower, as discussed earlier in Chapter 2.

Illus. 80. When carving a frame, use a hold-fast or clamp to secure the frame. Shown is a pattern being carved, first with a small, round rasp, followed by a round needle file. Finish with sandpaper and gild the grooves after painting the frame.

Remember to compensate for the width of the saw kerf in cutting the profile off the board. Always do this every time you make a cut of any kind. The saw kerf should be *outside* the measure, not included in it.

If you are mitring with a radial-arm saw, a mitre vise is a good invest-ment (Illus. 82–83). Such an arrangement is suitable for light mould-ings, and a hollow-ground mitre blade is recommended. Make the first mitre cut as shown in Illus. 82, to the right of the saw, and the second to the left, as in Illus. 83. Mouldings deeper than about 2 in (5.1 cm) should be cut with the mitre box.

Illus. 84 offers a design for making your own mitre jig, one that is suitable for use with the radial-arm saw. You can adapt the jig to use on a bench saw by making it wide enough to extend over both mitre-gauge slots in the table and attaching hardwood guide-bars to the bottom that slide in the slots.

Single-Board Profiles

Many moulding designs or profiles can be cut from single boards of various sizes. Select one of the numbered profiles between 1 and 20. You can use the same router bits and moulding cutters indicated in the text, or substitute others you may have on hand.

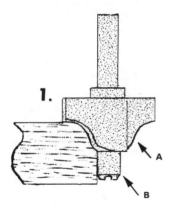

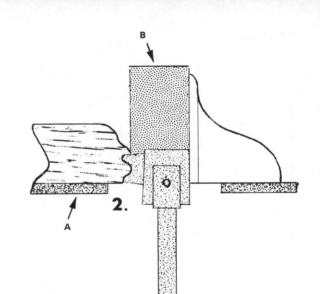

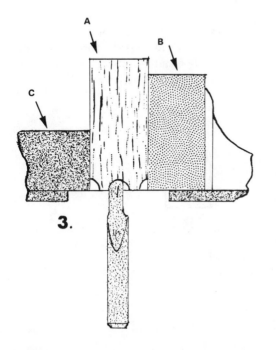

Illus. 81. 1. Guide the router bit, a ⁵⁄₃₂″ (4-mm) Roman ogee (A), with the pilot (B). Attach the router under the router table (A) and guide the wood into the revolving bit by the fence (B). 3. Attach the router again under the router table. Feed the wood (A) between the fence (B) and a guide board (C) clamped to the table.

1

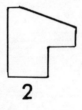

2

3

1. All cuts made with a saw.
2. All cuts made with a saw.

3. Cut 1—Roman ogee.
   Cut 2—$\frac{1}{4}''$ surface beading
   bit or $\frac{1}{4}''$ *bead*.

4

5

6

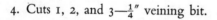

4. Cuts 1, 2, and 3—$\frac{1}{4}''$ veining bit.

5. Cut 1—$\frac{1}{8}''$ straight bit.
   Cuts 2 and 3—45° chamfer.
6. Cuts 1 and 2—rabbet bit.
   Cuts 3 and 4—chamfer.

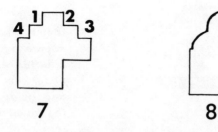

7　　　　　　**8**

7. Cuts 1, 2, 3, and 4—rabbet bit.
8. *Cloverleaf.*

9   10   11

9. Cut 1—cove part of $\frac{5}{32}$″ Roman ogee bit.
Cut 2—$\frac{3}{8}$″ cove bit.
10. Same as profile 9 but in reverse order.

11. Cut 1—cove of $\frac{5}{32}$″
Roman ogee bit.
Cut 2—$\frac{1}{4}$″ beading bit.

          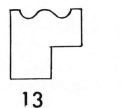   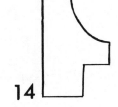

12   13   14

12. Same as profile 11,
but in reverse order.

13. $\frac{1}{4}$″ surface beading bit (or $\frac{1}{4}$″ *bead*).
14. $\frac{1}{2}$″ cove.

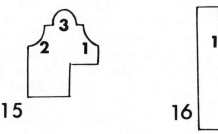 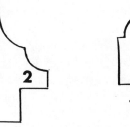 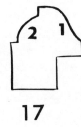

15   16   17

15. Cuts 1 and 2—half of $\frac{1}{4}$″ veiner ($\frac{3}{8}$″ deep, make
3 passes).
Cut 3—$\frac{1}{4}$″ *bead*.
16. Cuts 1 and 2—$\frac{5}{16}$″ *cove*.

17. Cut 1—$\frac{5}{32}$″ Roman ogee.
Cut 2—$\frac{1}{4}$″ beading bit.

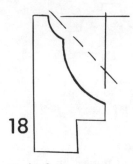

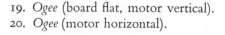

18. $\frac{1}{4}''$ *flute and* $\frac{1}{2}''$ *cove* (board flat on saw table, motor horizontal).

19. *Ogee* (board flat, motor vertical).
20. *Ogee* (motor horizontal).

When making deep shaping cuts, it is a good idea first to bevel off as much of the corner of the board as possible, by running it through the saw set at a 45° angle.

In the forthcoming profile drawings, an arrow or a blade outline indicates the long way of the moulding cutter on 45° cuts. All cuts are numbered; make cut #1 first, then #2, followed by #3 and so on. Names of moulding cutters are *italicized* so you can tell them at a glance from the router bits.

If you have trouble deciding how deep to make the cut, trace the outlines of the bits and cutters on heavy paper, cut them out and arrange them on a drawing of the proper-size board until they look like the profile drawings.

Under no circumstances attempt to make a full-depth cut at one pass with the moulding head. You may sometimes do this with the router, but if done with the moulding head, you run the risk of shattering the end of the board, and the board itself may be kicked back, so never stand directly behind it. (Keep the wood springs and hold-downs tight against the workpiece to help prevent this.) Wear work gloves with leather palms and also wear eye protection or a transparent face mask. These safety precautions are especially for the benefit of the beginner; hopefully, the experienced craftsman is well aware of them.

Make the cut in several passes, depending on its depth and how much physical contact the cutter makes with the wood. Usually $\frac{1}{32}$ in (1 mm) per pass is enough, though a first cut may sometimes be as deep as $\frac{1}{16}$ in

Illus. 82. A mitre vise used with the radial arm saw makes mitring easy. Make right-hand cut first.

Illus. 83. After you have cut all four mitres on the right-hand side, cut mitres to the left of the saw. Use a stop-block as shown to assure cutting opposite frame members the same length.

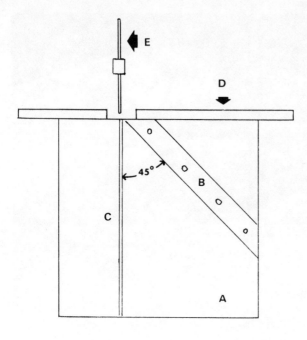

Illus. 84 (top right). Make your own mitring jig from a perfect square of ¾″ (19.1 mm) plywood (A). Glue and nail a piece of straight 1 × 2 (B) across one corner as shown. Be sure that it is evenly spaced so that it forms a 45° angle with the line of the saw cut (C). Clamp the jig to the table, flush against the saw fence (D). E indicates the saw blade. To cut left-handed mitres, turn the jig so that B is on the left-hand side.

(1.5 mm). Use a push-stick to push the moulding through and at the end of the pass, use a push-stick thin enough to pass under the revolving cutters (if there is no room on either side).

Standard sizes of lumber are used in the profiles unless stated otherwise. Illus. 103 clarifies routing with piloted bits and the router table, in case you are unfamiliar with these operations.

Compound Mouldings

Frames can be made larger and more elaborate by gluing two or more mouldings together. The separate boards are first worked to the profile desired, then glued and nailed together. Where nailing occurs, use brads of suitable length to leave at least ¼ in (6.4 mm) protruding, so that they can be pulled out after the glue has set. Fill the resulting holes with wood filler. If you are moulding a fine wood, such as Philippine mahogany, walnut or cherry that you will want simply to stain and varnish, avoid nails altogether. Or, drive them only in waste portions or from the bottom where the filled holes won't be visible at the back of the frame.

Starting with profile 21 through 31, the mouldings are composed of separate ¾-in (19-mm) boards, usually of stock width. If the bottom element of a compound moulding has a concave or convex undercut on the outer edge, opposite the rabbet, it may be difficult or impossible to hold it in a mitre vise or jig, or in a corner clamp. In this case, it is sometimes possible to cut and join (assemble) the bottom unit separately, then attach it to the joined upper frame with wood screws and glue. If this is not possible, attach to the bottom of each frame member, *with wood screws only,* an auxiliary strip of board or plywood about as wide as the overall width of the moulding and short enough not to get in the way of the mitre saw. Grip the moulding by the screwed-on strip when mitring and when joining the frame. Remove the strips after the frame has been assembled.

The dashed-line structure at the bottom of some profiles indicates an optional rabbet-forming strip that may be added when framing an oil or acrylic painting on stretched canvas. A solid outline indicates an integral part of the design.

PROFILES

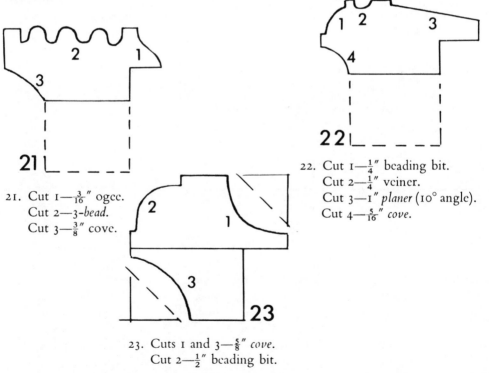

21. Cut 1—$\frac{3}{16}$″ ogee.
Cut 2—3-*bead.*
Cut 3—$\frac{3}{8}$″ cove.

22. Cut 1—$\frac{1}{4}$″ beading bit.
Cut 2—$\frac{1}{4}$″ veiner.
Cut 3—1″ *planer* (10° angle).
Cut 4—$\frac{5}{16}$″ *cove.*

23. Cuts 1 and 3—$\frac{5}{8}$″ *cove.*
Cut 2—$\frac{1}{2}$″ beading bit.

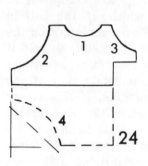
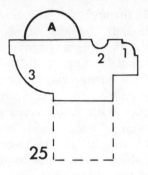
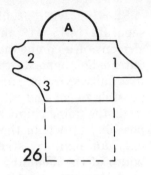

24. Cut 1—$\frac{1}{2}$″ core box bit.
Cut 2—$\frac{1}{2}$″ cove.
Cut 3—$\frac{5}{16}$″ *cove*.
Cut 4—$\frac{5}{8}$″ *cove*.

25. A—$\frac{3}{4}$″ half-round.
Cut 1—$\frac{1}{4}$″ beading bit.
Cut 2—$\frac{1}{4}$″ veiner.
Cut 3—$\frac{1}{2}$″ beading bit.

26. A—$\frac{3}{4}$″ half-round.
Cut 1—$\frac{3}{16}$″ ogee.
Cut 2—$\frac{1}{4}$″ surface beader.
Cut 3—$\frac{3}{8}$″ cove.

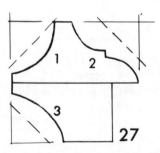
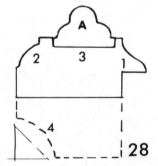

27. Cuts 1 and 3—$\frac{5}{8}$″ *cove*.
Cut 2—$\frac{5}{16}$″ *cove and bead*.

28. A—*cloverleaf* (glued in).
Cut 1—$\frac{3}{16}$″ ogee.
Cut 2—$\frac{1}{4}$″ beading bit.
Cut 3—groove $\frac{3}{4}$″ × $\frac{1}{4}$″ (made with dado head).
Cut 4—$\frac{1}{2}$″ cove.

29. Cut 1—1″ *flute* ($\frac{3}{16}$″ deep).
Cuts 2, 3 and 5—$\frac{5}{16}$″ cove.
Cut 4—rabbet.

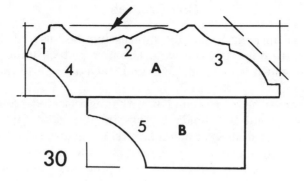

30. A—1 × 3.
    B—1 × 2.
    Cut 1—$\frac{1}{4}$″ beading bit.
    Cut 2—$\frac{5}{16}$″ *cove and bead* (45°).
    Cut 3—$\frac{5}{16}$″ *cove and bead* (motor vertical).
    Cut 4—$\frac{3}{8}$″ cove.
    Cut 5—$\frac{5}{8}$″ *cove.*

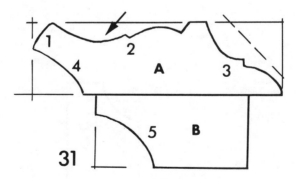

31. Cut 1—$\frac{1}{4}$″ corner round.
    Cut 2—$\frac{5}{16}$″ *cove and bead* (45°).
    Cut 3—$\frac{5}{16}$″ *cove and bead* (motor vertical).
    Cut 4—$\frac{1}{2}$″ cove.
    Cut 5—$\frac{5}{8}$″ *cove.*

Box Frames

Simple box frames are visually interesting because of the way they project the picture out from the wall. Use 1×2 stock lumber for the box part. If greater width is desired, you can attach a 1×3 to the bottom edge of the box.

Some box frames have a second box that is inserted from the back of the frame. The second box holds a glass in place and carries a piece of 3-dimensional art for display. Such a box frame is also called a shadow box.

Profiles 32 to 38 are all made with only the saw (plus a plane or sanding disk to smooth the cut edges). However, you may add decorative cuts with router bits and/or moulding cutters as you desire. Simple, straight-line mouldings such as these are severe enough for modern artwork, yet classic enough for representational art.

Profiles 32 and 33 are simple strip frames, without rabbet, designed for paintings on stretched canvas. Profiles 34–38 can be used for all types of artwork, as they have a rabbet lip for retaining glass and matted art.

PROFILES

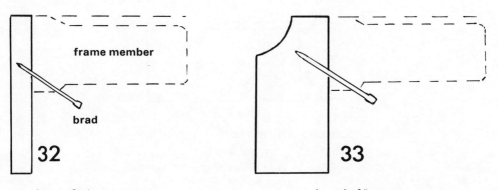

32. $\frac{1}{4}'' \times 1\frac{5}{8}''$ lattice strip.

33. 1×2 board; $\frac{3}{8}''$ cove.

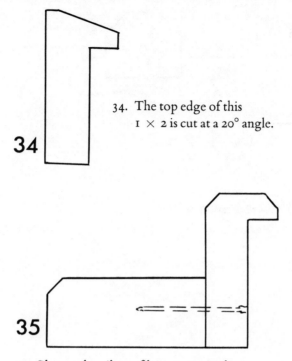

34. The top edge of this
1 × 2 is cut at a 20° angle.

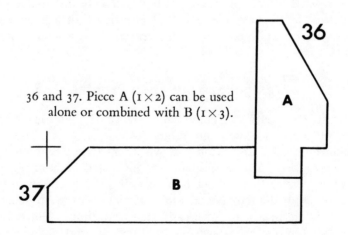

35. Glue and nail profile 34 to another 1 × 2.
All cuts are made with a chamfer bit or saw.

36 and 37. Piece A (1 × 2) can be used
alone or combined with B (1 × 3).

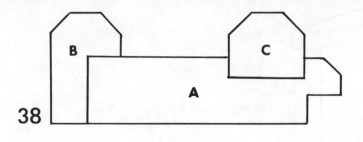

38. A—1×3.   C—$\frac{3}{4}'' \times \frac{5}{8}''$.
B—$\frac{3}{4}'' \times 1\frac{1}{4}''$.

This profile is only a suggestion of the many variations possible.

Flared Frames

Flared frames consist of two or more mouldings glued together, with one or more set at an angle, usually 45° for maximum depth of the frame and for ease of working the material. When properly finished (see Chapter 5), these frames lend great dignity and power to all kinds of art, from magnificent oil and acrylic paintings on stretched canvas to original prints and reproductions.

Designing Your Own Profiles

So you want to create a frame that bears the stamp of your own creativity! Well, here is how to go about it.

First decide how deep and wide you want the frame members to be. On a piece of paper, draw a cross-section of the board or boards you plan to use. Next, trace the outline of each moulding cutter and router bit onto heavy paper or 2-ply bristol board and cut them out with scissors *inside* the line so as to maintain accuracy of size and shape. Place the various cutouts on your lumber cross-section at varying angles and depths until you see the form you want taking shape (Illus. 85). Trace around the cutouts with a pencil, and that will be the outline of your profile. Transfer it with carbon paper to the end of the board and ink it in with a soft-tip pen. Use that as a guide in setting the cutters when moulding.

If you are making the same moulding cut on two or more boards, always run all the boards through on each pass. Don't finish one moulding and then try to make another just like it because it just won't work. The two mouldings may look alike, but you will never be able to make them match at the corners of the frame.

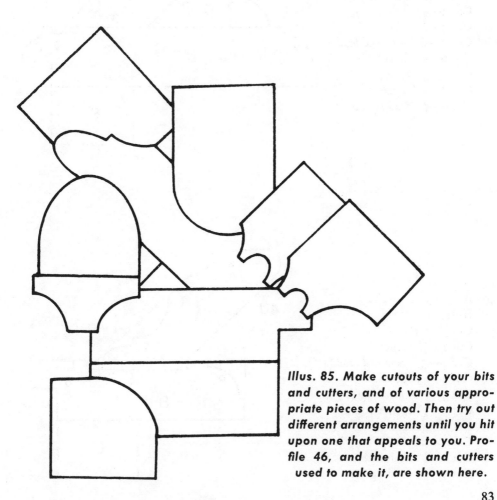

Illus. 85. Make cutouts of your bits and cutters, and of various appropriate pieces of wood. Then try out different arrangements until you hit upon one that appeals to you. Profile 46, and the bits and cutters used to make it, are shown here.

39. A—1×3.
    B—$\frac{3}{4}''$ half-round.
    C—$\frac{3}{4}'' \times 1\frac{1}{2}''$.
    D—1×4.
    E—$\frac{3}{4}'' \times 1''$.
    Cut 1—3-*bead*.
    Cut 2—$\frac{1}{4}''$ beading bit.
    Cut 3—45° bevel (A).
    Cut 4—$\frac{3}{8}''$ cove.
    Cut 5—$\frac{5}{16}''$ *cove and bead*.
    Cut 6—45° bevel.
    Cut 7—$\frac{1}{4}''$ veiner.
    Cut 8—$\frac{3}{16}''$ ogee.
    Cut 9—$\frac{3}{8}''$ beading bit.

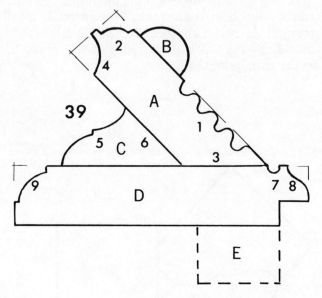

40. A—1×3.
    B—1×3.
    C—$\frac{3}{4}'' \times 1''$.
    Cut 1—$\frac{1}{4}''$ veiner.
    Cut 2—$\frac{5}{16}''$ *cove and bead* (45°).
    Cut 3—45° bevel.
    Cut 4—*base moulding* (15°).
    Cut 5—$\frac{1}{4}''$ corner round.
    Cut 6—groove $1\frac{1}{8}'' \times \frac{1}{8}''$.
    Cut 7—rabbet ($\frac{1}{8}'' \times \frac{1}{8}''$).
    Cut 8—$\frac{1}{8}''$ straight bit.
    Cut 9—$\frac{3}{8}''$ beading bit.

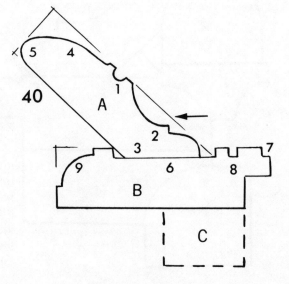

42. A—$\frac{3}{8}'' \times 1''$.
B—1×2.
C—1×2.
D—$\frac{3}{4}'' \times \frac{3}{4}''$.

41. A—1×4.   C—1×4.
B—1×2.   D—1×2.
Cut 1—$1''$ *flute* ($\frac{1}{4}''$ deep).
Cut 2—$1''$ *flute* ($\frac{1}{4}''$ deep, 3 passes—
shown by dotted line).
Cut 3—$\frac{5}{16}''$ *cove and bead* ($45°$).
Cuts 4 and 5—$\frac{5}{16}''$ *cove and bead*.
Cuts 6 and 7—$45°$ *bevel*.
Cut 8—$\frac{3}{16}''$ *ogee*.
Cut 9—$\frac{1}{2}''$ *beading bit*.
Cut 10—$1''$ *planer* ($15°$).

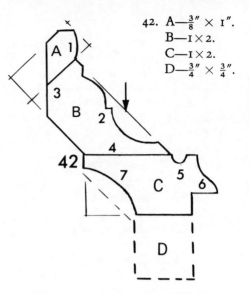

Cut 1—$\frac{1}{4}''$ *corner round*.
Cut 2—$\frac{5}{16}''$ *cove and bead* ($45°$).
Cuts 3 and 4—$45°$ *bevel*. (Put a
1×2 lift under moulding for
bevelling.)
Cut 5—$\frac{1}{4}''$ *veiner*.
Cut 6—$\frac{3}{16}''$ *ogee*.
Cut 7—$\frac{5}{8}''$ *cove*.

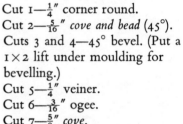

41

43. A—$\frac{3}{4}'' \times 3\frac{1}{8}''$.
B—$\frac{3}{4}'' \times 1\frac{7}{8}''$.
C—1×3.
D—$\frac{3}{4}'' \times 2\frac{1}{4}''$.
Cuts 1 and 2—$\frac{1}{4}''$ corner round.
Cuts 3 and 4—$\frac{5}{16}''$ *cove and bead* (45°).
Cut 5—$\frac{1}{2}''$ cove.
Cut 6—45° bevel.
Cut 7—$\frac{5}{8}''$ *cove*.
Cut 8—45° bevel.
Cut 9—$\frac{1}{4}''$ beading bit.
Cut 10—$\frac{3}{8}''$ beading bit.
Cut 11—$\frac{5}{8}''$ *cove*.

44. A—$\frac{3}{4}'' \times 1''$.
B—1×3.
C—*cloverleaf*.
D—corner of B.
E—1×3.
F—$\frac{3}{4}'' \times 2\frac{3}{8}''$.
Cut 1—$\frac{1}{4}''$ *bead* (45°).
Cut 2—$\frac{1}{4}''$ *flute* or $\frac{1}{4}''$ veiner.
Cut 3—*ogee*.
Cut 4—$1''$ *flute* (45°).
Cut 5—$\frac{5}{16}''$ *cove and bead*.
Cut 6—45° bevel.
Cut 7—$\frac{3}{8}''$ beading bit.
Cut 8—$\frac{1}{4}''$ beading bit.
Cut 9—$\frac{5}{16}''$ *cove and bead*.

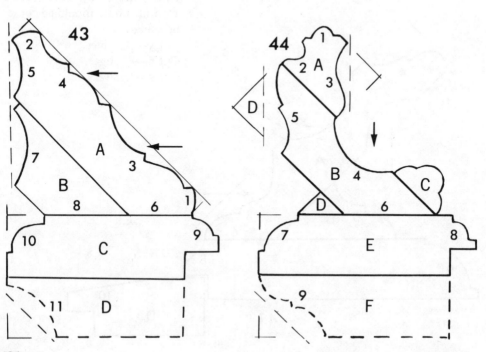

45. A—1×3.

B—$\frac{3}{4}'' \times 1\frac{1}{16}''$.

C—1×3.

D—1×3.

Cuts 1 and 2—$\frac{5}{16}''$ *cove and bead* (shown by dotted lines).

Cut 3—$45°$ bevel.

Cut 4—$\frac{5}{16}''$ *cove and bead*.

Cut 5—$\frac{5}{16}''$ *cove*.

Cut 6—$45°$ bevel.

Cut 7—$\frac{3}{8}''$ beading bit.

Cut 8—$\frac{1}{4}''$ surface beader.

Cuts 9 and 10—round off with file.

46. A—1×3.

B—waste triangle.

C—$\frac{3}{4}'' \times 2\frac{1}{4}''$.

D—$\frac{3}{4}'' \times 1\frac{7}{8}''$.

Cuts 1 and 2—$1''$ *flute* $(45°)$.

Cut 3—$\frac{1}{4}''$ *bead*.

Cut 4—$45°$ bevel.

Cut 5—$\frac{5}{16}''$ *cove and bead*.

Cut 6—$\frac{3}{8}''$ beading bit.

Cut 7—$\frac{1}{4}''$ *bead* $(45°)$.

Cut 8—$\frac{5}{8}''$ *cove*.

Cut 9—round off.

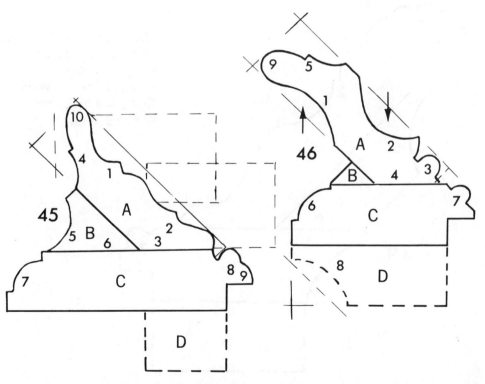

47. A—1×2.
 B—1×3.
 C—1×2.
 Cuts 1 and 2—$\frac{5}{8}''$ *cove.*
 Cuts 3, 4 and 5—$\frac{5}{16}''$ *cove and bead.*

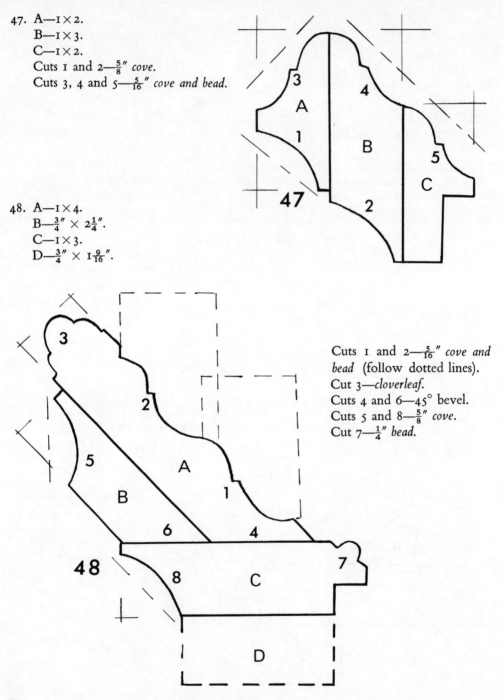

48. A—1×4.
 B—$\frac{3}{4}'' \times 2\frac{1}{4}''$.
 C—1×3.
 D—$\frac{3}{4}'' \times 1\frac{9}{16}''$.

Cuts 1 and 2—$\frac{5}{16}''$ *cove and bead* (follow dotted lines).
Cut 3—*cloverleaf.*
Cuts 4 and 6—45° *bevel.*
Cuts 5 and 8—$\frac{5}{8}''$ *cove.*
Cut 7—$\frac{1}{4}''$ *bead.*

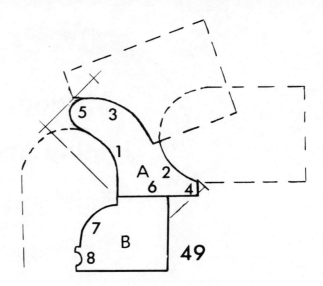

Cuts 1 and 2—1″ *flute* (follow dotted lines).
Cut 3—*base moulding* (25°).
Cut 4—45° bevel.
Cut 5—bevel and round off.
Cut 6—45° bevel.
Cut 7—$\frac{3}{8}$″ beading bit.
Cut 8—$\frac{1}{8}$″ veiner.

49. A—1 × 2.
    B—$\frac{3}{4}$″ × 1″.

Making, Joining and Finishing Frames

Round, Oval and Odd-Shaped

Round and oval frames, or frames having a curved part, often are used for mirrors as well as pictures. These odd-shaped frames add a designer touch to home or office.

To make any round frame up to about 11 in (28 cm) in diameter—or equal to the widest board you can find—draw the outer circle on a board with a compass. Reduce the radius by the width of the frame and draw the inner circle. Cut out the ring and work it as described below.

Round Frames

Small, round frames can be lathe-turned, but to make larger frames, construct an octagon (an 8-sided figure) out of 1 × 4 or wider lumber. You can cut a ring up to 1¾ in (4.4 cm) wide from a 1 × 4, the maximum ring-width being equal to ½ the width of the octagon segment.

The length of side S (Illus. 86) is found by multiplying the radius of the outside circle by .828. For instance, for a 14-in (35.6-cm) circle having a 7-in radius R (17.8-cm), figure .828 × 7 (17.8) = 5.8 in. Round off to 5½ in (14 cm) for easier handling. Add ½ in (12.7 mm) for the lap joint at one end (it is included in the length on the other end) where the segments are glued together. To provide sawing room outside the circle, add another ½ in (12.7 mm) to the length of each segment (side). This will let the circle fall inside the octagon for truer cutting. With the mitre box set at 22.5°, cut the 8 pieces, each 6½ in (16.5 cm) long on the longer side. When cutting flat lumber, you need not swing the saw to cut the second angle; just turn the board over. Cut the ½-in (12.7-mm) lap joints on top at one end and on the bottom at the other end of each segment. Assemble the octagon on a flat surface with glue and weight down until set. *Use no nails in the joints!* Transfer the inner and outer circles to the wood and cut the frame ring. True up the inside circle with a sanding drum, the outside with a disk.

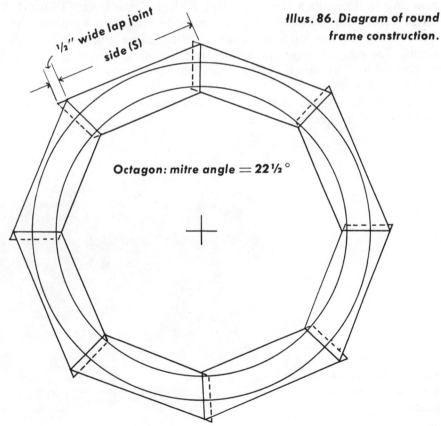

Illus. 86. Diagram of round frame construction.

½″ wide lap joint

side (S)

Octagon: mitre angle = 22½°

For routing, the ring must be firmly clamped to the table with a surface clamp (Illus. 87), or to the table edged with a C-clamp. You minimize the risk of chipping the mitre joints by moving the router around the inner circle in a *counterclockwise* direction. To further minimize the risk, cut the rabbet first, using a $\frac{5}{16}$-in (8-mm) rabbeting bit. Don't hog out the entire cut in one pass, but make at least three passes to rabbet to a depth of $\frac{5}{16}$ in (8 mm). Make each pass from one side of the clamp around the circle to the other side, then reclamp in a new place and rout the remainder of the pass.

Turn the ring over, change bits and shape the rabbet lip from the front with a Roman ogee or other bit, moving the router *counterclockwise* around the circle. Change bits to a cove or quarter-round and shape the outside edge of the ring, moving the router *clockwise* this time.

If you are making a deep cut on the outside, as with a ½-in (12.7-mm) bead-and-quarter-round bit, make at least three passes, but if the ring is no more than ¾ in (19 mm) thick, the pilot will run into the table top, scarring it. So make a lift by cutting a circle from ¾-in (19-mm) plywood ½ in (12.7 mm) smaller than the outside ring. Cut another circle ½ in (12.7 mm) smaller than the inside of the frame and nail it to the larger circle. The ring fits over the smaller circle and the whole set-up is clamped to the table. The small circle gives the router a surface to ride on and keeps it from tilting.

Smooth the shaped surface with medium-grit (150) sandpaper to de-emphasize the grain of the wood.

Illus. 87. First router cut on a round frame is the rabbet.

92

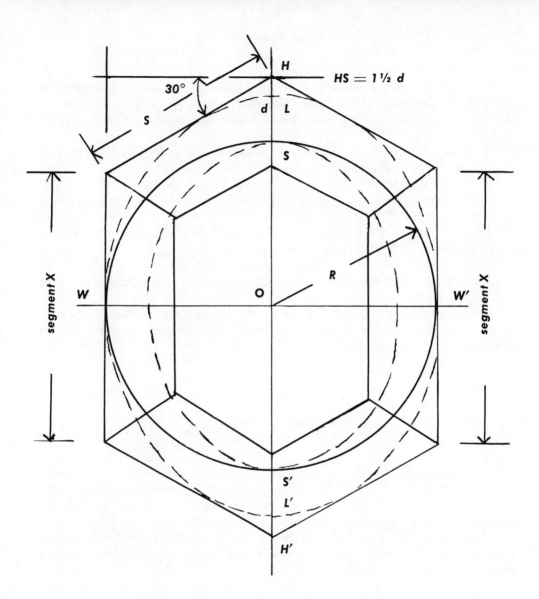

Illus. 88. Diagram of oval frame construction.

Oval Frames

The wooden figure from which an oval frame is cut has the shape of a "stretched" hexagon (Illus. 88). The most pleasing proportions for an oval frame are 2:3, 3:4 and 4:5. The diagram shows an oval with a ratio of 4:5.

To figure the length of the side S, multiply the radius of the circle R (½ the width of the oval) by 1.155.

The length of each of the two "stretched" sides (segment X) is equal to S + D, where D equals the difference in length between the major and minor axes of the ellipse. Example: where the width = 8 in (20.3 cm) and the length = 10 in (25.4 cm), the difference D is 10 in (25.4 cm) minus 8 in (20.3 cm) = 2 in (5.1 cm).

Set the saw at 30° on the mitre box and cut four segments S + ½ in (12.7 mm) (for the lap joints), and two segments measuring S + ½ in (12.7 mm) + D.

Cut the lap joints, glue and assemble the segments, transfer the ellipses to the figure, cut out the elliptical ring and continue working the frame as described for a round one.

Odd-Shaped Frames

An equilateral triangle, a pentagon, hexagon, octagon or any other figure with straight sides can be built up of segments cut from pre-fabricated moulding. Illus. 89 provides a table of cutting angles for regular polygons, and Illus. 90 shows a few of the many possible figures you can construct. However, if the frame is partly curved and partly straight (as a rectangle topped by a semicircle), the whole frame must be worked as if it were a circle.

To make a frame in the shape of an equilateral triangle requires setting the saw to an angle of 60°—an impossibility as the mitre-box swing does not go beyond 45°. So take a sliding "T" bevel and adjust it to a 60° angle by holding it against a protractor, and transfer the angle to the board or moulding for cutting. Adjust the saw to a 45° position, place the moulding with one edge touching the mitre-box fence, and line up the cutting mark with the sawteeth (Illus. 91). Clamp the board to the mitre-box bed and saw the mitre.

Name	Mitre box angle	No. sides
equilateral triangle	60°	3
pentagon	36°	5
hexagon	30°	6
heptagon	25.83°	7
octagon	22.5°	8
decagon	18°	10
dodecagon	15°	12

Illus. 89. Table of Regular Polygons.

Joining or Assembling Frames

For putting the frame together, you need a work table, four corner clamps, glue, a nail set with a 1/32-in (1-mm) tip, hand drill, brads 1½ in to 2 in (3.8–5.1 cm) long—depending on the width of the frame—and a hammer. Glue a frame member (Illus. 92) and clamp it in a corner clamp with its adjacent frame member. Adjust until the mitres match perfectly, then tighten both sides of the clamp. If the frame is too wide to be held in a corner clamp, make a jig like that shown in Illus. 93. Continue around the frame, glueing and clamping each corner. Nail from one side only (Illus. 94). The nails hold the corner together until the glue has a chance to set. A heavy frame can be nailed from both sides of each corner. Set the nailheads about ⅛ in (3.2 mm) below the surface (Illus. 95) and fill the holes with wood filler. Sand smooth when dry.

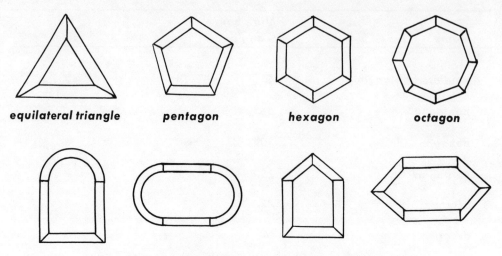

equilateral triangle   pentagon   hexagon   octagon

Illus. 90. Some regularly and irregularly shaped frames.

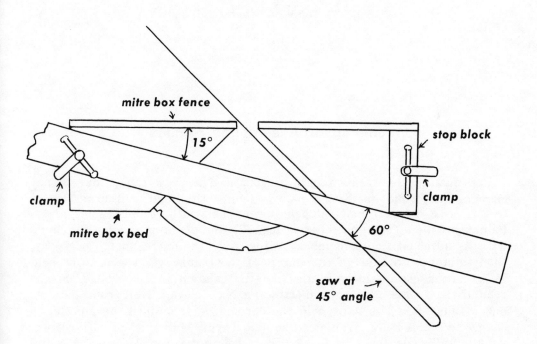

Illus. 91. How to adjust moulding in mitre box for 60° cut.

Illus. 92. Apply glue to mitred end of one piece of moulding and clamp it to its matching piece in a corner clamp. Glue and clamp together all the pieces at the same time, in the same way.

Illus. 93. If frame is too wide for corner clamps, make a jig like the one shown. Clamp small boards at ends of mouldings, or, if possible, clamp moulding itself. Use pads to avoid marring. Then glue and nail the ends together.

Illus. 94. When nailing, either vertically or horizontally, always brace the opposite corner against something—either as shown or against a board clamped to the table.

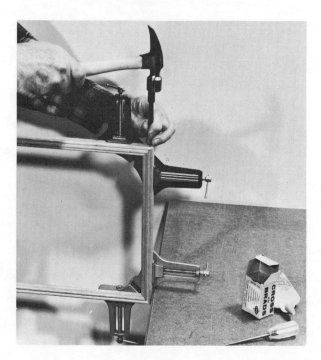

Illus. 95. Use a nail set with a ⅟₃₂″ (1 mm) tip to drive the nail below the surface. Drive it in far enough so that wood filler will not fall out.

Prefinishing

Carving

A picture frame is almost always enhanced by carving, a technique that need not be complex or overpowering (Illus. 96). You can make an attractive carving on your frame with nothing but equally spaced notches cut in with a file.

After assembly, mark out the carving and work it up (Illus. 97). If you carve the moulding before mitring it, measure the cuts with extreme care so the design will match at the corners (Illus. 36).

Much carving can be done with rasps and smoothed with files. Illus. 98 shows how to make a jig for holding half-round and cloverleaf mouldings while file-carving. With experience, you can even carve a leaf pattern or some vines with regular tools.

To make a frame look old, "distress" the surface—that is, before finishing, scrape and scratch the wood with the point of an awl or a broken piece of a bandsaw or hacksaw blade gripped in the jaws of a locking plier.

Frame Inserts

Fabric-covered inserts buffer the artwork from direct contact with the frame. Suitable fabrics are decorator burlap (hessian) from a fabric store or the variety store, or unbleached linen canvas from an art supply dealer.

Study the frames you see in art shop windows and plan your inserts accordingly. Make an insert from stock 1 × 2 lumber. Construct the insert to fit the art or mat, and the frame to fit the insert. Select the cover fabric and cut it into strips about 2 in (5.1 cm) wider and longer than the corresponding sides of the insert (Illus. 99A).

Now, brush a thin coat of white glue on one long side, let it get tacky, then lay on the fabric and pat it down. Too much glue will strike through the cloth and spoil it, so be careful. Glue and cover the opposite long side, then the two short sides. Before the glue is entirely dry, locate the inside and outside corners and mark them on the fabric with a pencil. Take a metal straightedge and a mat knife or razor blade and cut each mitre through both layers of cloth (Illus. 99B). Discard the cut-off ends and rub the unglued ends of fabric down into the partially set glue at the mitres. When it is fully dry, trim off the excess fabric around the insert with scissors (Illus. 100). Then turn the insert over, brush glue on the lip of the rabbet and rub the cloth down. When this is dry, run your knife down the corner of the rabbet, cutting out the excess fabric (Illus. 99C).

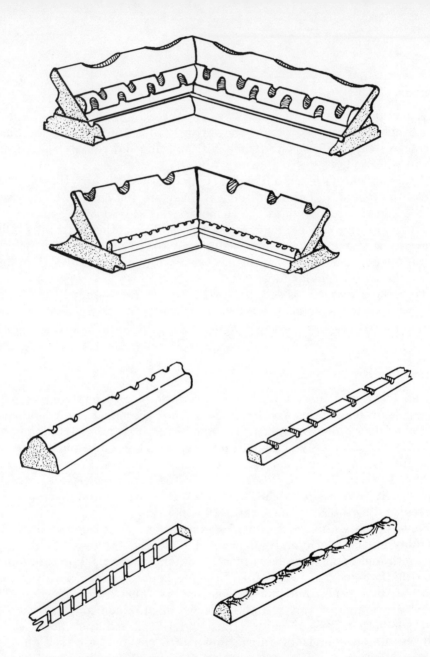

Illus. 96. Carving frames with files offers many possibilities for design. Edges can be wavy or scalloped, and beads and other cuts carved in a variety of ways (right).

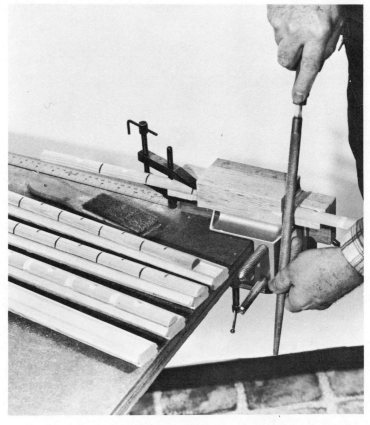

Illus. 97. The jig diagrammed in Illus. 98 is here used for carving a half-round to be glued into a groove cut with a dado in the moulding. Plan carving carefully, taking into account the mitre cuts, to assure that the carving will be symmetrical on the finished frame.

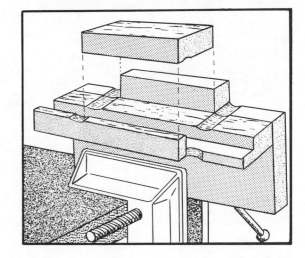

Illus. 98. Use a holding jig such as this (also shown in Illus. 36) to carve pieces before assembly of the frame. The jig shown here is made of pieces 1 × 2 and 1 × 4, nailed and glued together.

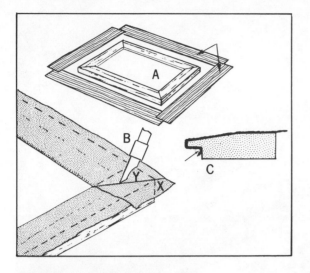

Illus. 99. Follow these steps when covering an insert. Make sure that you don't put too much glue on the insert, or it will ruin the cloth.

Illus. 100. Trim the excess cloth from the outside edges with scissors.

Fillets

A fillet is a narrow insert that may be used in place of the regular insert, or in conjunction with it, next to the artwork. The best way to finish the fillet is to gild it, either with gold paint or metal-leafing, a process soon to be described.

Finishing Frames

First fill all nail holes and cracks with plastic wood filler or water putty. Sand with coarse garnet paper when dry. Round off corners and sharp edges with a grit file or sandpaper on a block. Use a round or half-round file for cove corners (Illus. 101). Leave the surface a little rough for gessoing, but sand it smooth if you are staining and lacquering or varnishing the frame.

Illus. 101. Round off all corners and sharp edges with a file, then smooth with coarse garnet paper.

Stained Frames

Wood stains are excellent for Philippine mahogany and hardwood frames. Water stain is cleaner to handle than oil stain, but you will have to sand after it dries because it raises the grain. You can also use one of the newer, rapid-drying vinyl stains.

Apply the stain with a narrow brush, according to the width of the frame (Illus. 102). When it is dry, sand lightly, dust off and apply several coats of a clear, lacquer-type finish such as Deft, following the directions on the can. Softwoods are seldom attractive with a stained finish and look infinitely better with an opaque finish. Narrow frames are often painted matte black, edged with a stripe of gold paint. Or, they may be painted white or some other color.

Rub down the final coat of a clear finish with #000 steel wool, then polish with a paste floor wax preferably containing carnauba wax. Do not wax open-grain woods such as Philippine mahogany, as the wax plugs up the grain and shows speckled white.

Painted and Textured Frames

An elaborate frame often looks attractive with an elaborate finish. Creative use of acrylic polymer painting materials such as artists use will give your frame an interesting finish that will complement the art.

◆ *Finishing Materials.* You need a can of acrylic gesso, a can of acrylic modelling paste, a bottle of acrylic matte medium (varnish), and such acrylic tube colors as red oxide (bole), burnt umber, utramarine blue, chrome oxide green, yellow ochre, Mars black, etc. (*Never use oil paints in combination with acrylics.*)

For smooth paintings of colors, use acrylic brushes with gold-color bristles ¼ in (6.3 mm), ⅜ in (9.5 mm), ½ in (17.7 mm), ¾ in (19 mm) and 1 in (25.7 mm) wide, and a 1½ in (3.8 cm) sash-painting brush. For applying gold paint, have on hand several narrow widths of flat red-sable brushes and a #6 and a #10 round red sable brush as well. For dry-brushing and daubing on thick layers of modelling paste, use hog-bristle brushes #2 and #4 long and #5 and #8 bright (short).

Acrylic gesso is a thick, white paint composed of titanium white pigment and calcium, magnesium and aluminum carbonates and silicates in acrylic medium. You can create attractive, interesting textures in thick gesso by running the teeth of a coarse comb (broken off a combination comb) through it when it has stiffened but not fully set.

Gesso, painted on thickly, retains brush marks that are difficult to sand

Illus. 102. Give the entire frame a coat of stain of desired color. To make it darker, apply more coats. Light toned woods look best with a dark stain.

out, so, for a smooth surface, thin with ⅓ water and apply three or more coats to the wood until the grain is hidden. Sand only the last coat. Paint over this base with gesso mixed with a little black to form a dark grey tone. This makes a neutral base for the colors that will be painted over it. You can also make grey tones by mixing complementary colors with the gesso (red and green, yellow and violet, blue and orange, etc.). Gesso can be colored as desired by adding any acrylic color.

Acrylic modelling paste is a white compound like gesso, but thickened with marble dust or carbonates. You use it to achieve heavy textures. It makes an attractive foundation for gold paint.

Principles of Frame Painting

A frame must be painted with colors that harmonize with those in the painting. The general tone may be the same as the main color in the

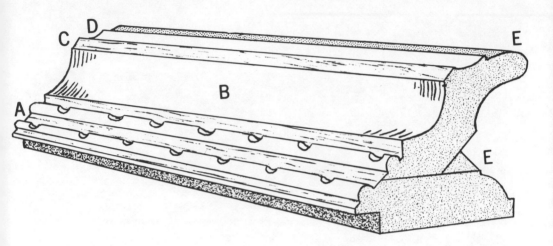

Illus. 103. Paint profile 46 following this cross-section. (See P. 87).

painting or complementary to it. If you are matching the main color, grey the frame color by adding a little black or its complementary color. Add gesso to lighten.

Finishing the Frame

Profile 46 has been taken as a general example of finishing (Illus. 103). Other profiles can be finished in a similar way. Variations of color and harmony are infinite, however, so experiment—don't just use this one method of working for all your frames.

First seal the back and the rabbet (parts to be left without other finish) with a coat of matte acrylic medium. Acrylic paints and mediums are self-priming and can be applied directly to the raw wood. Next apply gesso to the frame as discussed above (Illus. 104). For a smooth finish that does not show brush marks, use a mixture of 2/3 gesso thinned with ⅓ water. Let each coat dry before applying the next, and continue with coats until the wood grain no longer shows through. Sand the last coat with #220 garnet paper and polish with #000 steel wool.

Apply a thick, textured coat of modelling paste to surface *D* (Illus. 103). Daub it into the gully with a hog-bristle brush (Illus. 105). When this has dried, paint the front and sides of the frame with a coat of dark grey gesso. Smooth with steel wool when dry.

Illus. 104. Apply two or more coats of gesso as it comes from the can, or thin with up to ⅓ cup of water and paint on more coats for easier sanding and a smoother finish.

Illus. 105. Daub on modelling paste with a short hog-bristle artist's brush.

Paint surface D and the bottom part of surface A (rabbet lip) with red oxide (Illus. 106). Thin the paint with a little water. Paint surface E (top edge and sides of frame) with medium grey gesso.

Brush a thick coat of light grey gesso over surface B and the upper part of surface A. Allow it to dry a little on surface B until it thickens, then brush on another thick coat and let that thicken for about 10 minutes. Then take the coarse end of a broken comb and comb through the soft gesso to the hard, dark grey gesso underneath (Illus. 107), creating a two-tone pattern of ridges.

Apply a suitable acrylic color (the main color of the painting, subdued and greyed) to surface E, or just leave it grey. Dip a long hog-bristle brush in the same color, wipe off the excess on a paper towel, and dry-brush surface B with streaks and flecks of color. Make sure the ridged gesso is dry before you dry-brush it. Now take a color complementary to the first, tone it down with a little black, and dry-brush it sparingly on the inside and outside of the frame.

Brush gold paint on the surfaces previously painted with red oxide

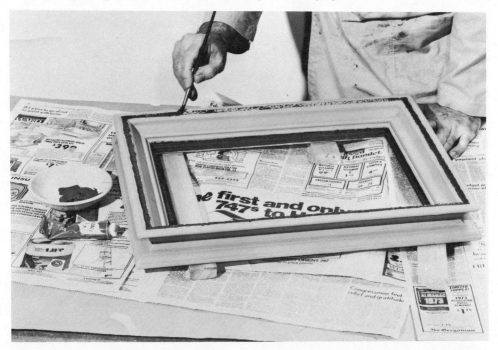

Illus. 106. Paint a thick coat of red oxide over the dried modelling paste and the first bead at the bottom of the frame. The red oxide warms the tone of the gold paint applied over it.

(Illus. 108), using a red-sable brush. Allow flecks of the red to show through. You can buy gold paint ready-made or make your own by stirring bronze powder into bronzing liquid or acrylic medium thinned slightly with water. After the gold paint has dried, go over it lightly with steel wool, rubbing through here and there until a few streaks of red and grey show up. Don't overdo it. With a hog-bristle brush, dry-brush the inner and outer surfaces of the frame *very lightly* with gold paint. If you happen to apply too much, just sand it off when dry.

Finally, sand surface *E* in a few scattered spots and edges to expose the underlying grey tones.

When the entire frame is dry, polish lightly with #000 steel wool and varnish with a mixture of two parts matte medium to one part water. It goes on milky looking, but dries clear.

Varnishing not only protects the paint, but also keeps the gold color from tarnishing. Polish the finished frame with a paste floor wax containing carnauba wax. (The finished frame is in Illus. 109.)

Illus. 107. Comb ridges through the soft, thick gesso with a broken piece of coarse comb. This provides an interesting texture and enhances the appearance of the frame.

Antiquing a Frame

Frames with light and medium yellow-grey or green-grey tones look attractive when antiqued. The antiquing should be done before the final varnishing. Mottle the finish by applying one part burnt umber mixed with four parts of matte acrylic medium. Brush it on quickly and—just as quickly—wipe it off with a soft cloth or tissue, leaving dark tones in the corners and deep parts of any carving. Go over the frame as many times as is necessary to make it look right. Let dry and dry-brush with tints of red oxide and gold paint. Illus. 110, 111, 112 show antiqued and gilt frames.

Illus. 108. Brush on gold paint (bronze powder in acrylic medium) over the red oxide.

Spatter

Spattering is another technique to make a frame look old. Appropriate colors are black, burnt umber, burnt sienna, Hooker's green, ultramarine blue, etc. Mix a little color and plenty of water in a saucer. Dip a not-too-stiff toothbrush (or other rather stiffish brush) into the color. Shake off the excess by striking the brush handle against a stick of wood held over newspaper. When the color begins to spatter, strike the brush over the frame. Repeat as necessary to get the effect desired. If too much goes on, wipe off immediately with a wet rag, let dry, and try again. You can use only black, or combine several colors.

Illus. 109. This is the finished frame. There is an infinite number of variations on this method, so don't confine yourself to the colors and method described here.

Illus. 110. Double-matted block print in color on 100 percent rag paper. Bottom mat is museum board, top mat standard matboard, gold color. Frame 13 × 17″ (33 × 43.2 cm), similar to Profile 11, antique green. Outside cove textured with acrylic modelling paste and painted over the red oxide under gold paint. Frame 1½″ (3.8 cm) deep.

Illus. 111. A ready-made frame, carved and finished with wax-gilt.

Illus. 112. Profile 29 provides an attractive 17 × 21″ (43.1 × 53.3 cm) frame for this 14 × 18″ (35.6 × 45.7 cm) oil painting. Note combing of the gesso and gilt over modelling paste in the gully.

Wax Gilding

The simplest finish for a frame is merely bronze powder mixed with wax. Bronze powder comes in several shades of gold, as well as pewter, antique copper, red, green and blue. For a gold finish, prepare the frame with gesso and brush on a coat of red oxide. Let dry. Knead bronze powder into a lump of paste floor wax containing carnauba wax. Spread it over the frame with your fingers or a soft rag. If the color goes on too thin in spots, sprinkle on some of the same powder and rub it in until the color is smooth and even. Allow the wax to dry, then polish with a soft cloth. Varnish with matte acrylic medium thinned slightly with water.

For variation, omit red oxide and substitute a coat of red bronzing powder in wax. Let dry, polish, and apply wax gilt in a shade of gold or some other color. Polish and varnish.

Refinishing Old Frames

If an old frame is too weak and wobbly for the mitres to be firmed up by stapling (Illus. 113), carefully take it apart, clean the old glue from the mitre joints, reglue and nail back together. If part of the carving is missing, replace it by first sanding off the old finish to the bare wood, then applying modelling paste. Build it up in several ⅛ in- (3.2 mm-) coats to the required height, waiting for each coat to dry before applying the next. When it is dry, carve it with a knife or rifflers and files to match the rest of the decoration. In refinishing a frame, first sand off as much of the old finish as you can (don't try to get down into every crack and crevice), then refinish with gesso and paints as described.

Metal Leafing

Metal-leafing kits containing imitation gold leaf, gold size such as the professionals use, and complete instructions are widely available and are recommended. Real gold leaf is too expensive and difficult to handle for the beginner.

Another way to metal-leaf a fillet or frame is to use matte acrylic medium for an adhesive. Prepare the frame with gesso and sand it *smooth*. Whether you metal-leaf the entire frame or just certain areas is a matter of choice. Paint the desired surface with red oxide for imitation gold, or with Mars black for imitation silver (aluminum) leaf.

Paint one side of the frame with slightly thinned acrylic medium and let it sit for a few minutes to get a little tacky. Open the book of imitation gold to the first leaf and lift up the paper it rests on. With scissors, cut a strip of the foil slightly wider than the width of the space you are gilding.

Illus. 113. Staples across the mitres of wide frames add extra security and will tighten slightly loose corners of old frames.

Cut through paper and all. Take the metal leaf in your fingers (impossible with real gold leaf) and lay it carefully on the treated frame. Pat it down with a small wad of cotton. Cut a second strip and lay it on, overlapping the first one about ¼ in (6.4 mm). Continue around the frame, varnishing each side with acrylic medium and letting it get tacky before leafing. Don't worry if you tear holes in the leaf or if the red oxide shows through; just cut another strip of leaf and press it down over the damage.

Wait a couple of hours until the medium is entirely dry, then carefully rub the gilt with cotton or a soft cloth to remove all superfluous leaf. If you want an antique gold effect, add a little orange and/or yellow ochre, with maybe a touch of black, to the medium, or use burnt umber instead, and brush it on and wipe it off as in regular frame antiquing. When dry, varnish with matte medium.

Hanging Pictures

After you have constructed, assembled, fitted and finished your framing project, it's time to hang your artwork. You can hang pictures singly or group them in any one of a number of interesting ways, depending on the size, shape and number of framed pictures involved. Illus. 114 shows several ways an odd assortment of pictures can be balanced through proper hanging.

To hang a picture straight the first time, hold a small level against the top of the frame. When the bubble centers in the vial, the picture is hanging straight.

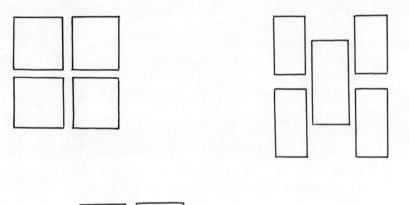

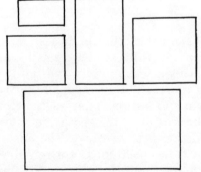

Illus. 114. Seek a balanced arrangement in your display of framed pictures. Your own eye is the sole judge, as balance depends on size and number of framed pictures and the amount of space you have to fill.

Wiring the Frame

Choose a strength of wire suitable for the weight of the frame and its contents. Illus. 115 shows the back of a small frame with screw eyes installed about one-fourth of the frame width down from the top. The closer you put these to the middle, the more the frame will lean outward from the wall. Be careful about placing them too high, as the wire and hanger are likely to show above the frame if you do.

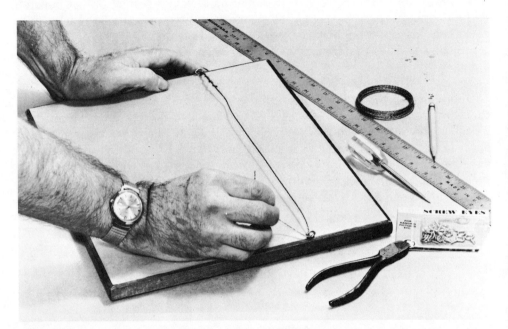

Illus. 115. Wrap wire around shank of screw eye, then back around itself to secure. Heavy frames require second part of screw eyes in bottom edge of frame—insurance in case either of upper screw eyes pulls out. Note Kraft paper dust seal glued to frame.

Cut the wire 6 in to 8 in (15.2–20.3 cm) longer than the space between the screw eyes. Pass one end through the eye, wrap it once around the shank of the screw eye, then back around itself, as shown. Pull the wire straight across; don't leave it slack—it will slacken enough of its own accord. Wrap the other end of the wire in the same way.

Wrapping the wire around the shanks of the screw eyes will keep it from eventually slipping out and allowing the picture to fall. Always use stranded picture wire, never solid wire, which grows brittle with movement and easily breaks. If you are hanging a heavy frame, do not depend on two opposed screw eyes. As the wood dries out, the pull of the wire will cause the screw eyes to loosen and, unless detected in time, to pull out completely and let the framed picture drop, possibly suffering irreparable damage.

To avoid this possibility, turn a second pair of screw eyes into the bottom edge of the frame. Start wiring from one of these screw eyes, fix the wire into the upper screw eye, then across to the other (wrapping as directed above to prevent slipping), then down to the other bottom screw eye where the end of the wire is made fast. Now if one of the upper screw eyes pulls out, you will be warned of it by the awkward hang of the picture and can remedy the situation before it goes any further. The following are some sample frames, from simple to complex.

Illus. 116. These frames are constructed (left to right, top to bottom) from profile 39 (page 84), profile 44 (page 86), profile 41 (page 85), profile 26 (page 78), and, inside profile 26, profile 28 (page 78).

Illus. 117. A 6 × 8″ (15 × 20.3 cm) oil landscape in a frame 12½″ × 14½ × 2½″ (32 × 37 × 6.3 cm) deep. Profile 39. The back of the frame is wider than the front, and an effect of double framing is achieved.

Illus. 118. A small painting (5 × 7″ or 12.7 × 17.8 cm) gains strength with a relatively wide frame. Texturing, gilding and antiquing lead the eye into the picture.

Illus. 119. A trio of related paintings can be hung in this way for a balanced effect, or strung out in a horizontal or vertical line. Small paintings like these (8 × 10″ or 20.3 × 25.4 cm) achieve importance when projected from the wall by a box frame.

Illus. 120. Colored lithograph mounted in a museum board mat, painted with gilt around the window. Second mat covered with dark green velvet to set off the bright red of the mushrooms. A narrow mat of gilt color separates the velvet from the glass.

Illus. 121. This etching on 100 percent rag paper is mounted with cream-colored museum board. Frame is 12 × 15″ (30.5 × 38 cm), router profiled in Philippine mahogany.

Metric Conversion Chart

$\frac{1}{8}$ inch = 3.18 millimetres $\frac{5}{8}$ inch = 15.88 millimetres $1\frac{1}{2}$ inch = 38.10 millimetres

$\frac{1}{4}$ inch = 6.35 millimetres $\frac{3}{4}$ inch = 19.05 millimetres   2 inches = 50.80 millimetres

$\frac{3}{8}$ inch = 9.53 millimetres $\frac{7}{8}$ inch = 22.23 millimetres   1 foot = 30.48 centimetres

$\frac{1}{2}$ inch = 12.70 millimetres   1 inch = 25.40 millimetres   1 yard = 0.9144 metre

10 millimetres = 1 centimetre

Index